VANGUARD SERIES

EDITOR: MARTIN WINDROW

GW00537437

The CENTURION TANK in Battle

Text by
SIMON DUNSTAN

Colour plates by
PETER SARSON, TONY BRYAN
and
DAVID E. SMITH

OSPREY PUBLISHING LONDON

Published in 1981 by
Osprey Publishing Ltd
59 Grosvenor Street, London W1X 9DA
© Copyright 1981 Osprey Publishing Ltd
Reprinted 1986, 1987, 1988, 1989, 1991

To Edward

Cover painting : Centurion Mk 5 of 'A' Sqn., 6th Royal
Tank Rgt.; Suez, November 1956. See Plates
commentaries for full details.

ISBN 0 85045 398 4

Filmset in Great Britain
Printed in Hong Kong through Bookbuilders Ltd

An Auster AOP Mk.6 flies over Centurions Mk.2 of 11th Armoured Division on the tank training grounds at Hohne in West Germany, 1952. For 25 years Centurion was the main battle tank of the British Army, and remains in frontline service with several armies around the world. (Soldier)

Introduction

It is curious that the British, who have traditionally held the horse in high esteem, should twice in their history have produced the weapon that diminished the rôle of that animal on the battlefield. The Welsh longbow at Crécy and Agincourt decimated the mounted knights of the Middle Ages. Five hundred years later, once again on the battlefields of France, another British innovation superseded cavalry entirely – the tank. No tank has proved more successful than the Centurion.

Conceived in the closing stages of the Second World War, Centurion arrived too late to see action against the German Panzers that had dominated that conflict. Although designed for warfare in Europe, it was not until 1951 that Centurion first saw combat in a completely different theatre – the rugged hills of Korea. It was not a fair proving ground for any tank, but in the words of the then-Director of the Royal Armoured Corps, 'the Centurion was tested to the full and not found wanting'. Its impressive performance under difficult conditions led to many overseas sales and Centurion was destined to fight its major campaigns in the hands of foreign armies.

As with all successful tank designs, Centurion combined the three principal attributes of the AFV – firepower, mobility and armour protection – to a high degree. Due to the soundness of the

original design it was possible to improve all these features repeatedly whilst ensuring that Centurion remained a relatively simple tank to operate. In battle its reliability, firepower and ability to withstand punishment have found favour with all who have served in 'Cents'. The technical development of Centurion has been related elsewhere. The aim of this monograph is to recount some of the exploits of this outstanding tank in combat.

Korea 1950–1953

The Centurion first saw combat during the Korean War under conditions that could hardly have been less suitable for the employment of tanks. The steep hills and glutinous rice paddies were often impassable, while primitive roads and flimsy bridges severely restricted the movement of heavy armour.

The 8th King's Royal Irish Hussars, equipped with three squadrons of Centurions Mark 3 and a Reconnaissance Troop of Cromwells, landed at Pusan on 14 November 1950 as armour support to 29th British Independent Brigade. After an uncomfortable journey north on the delapidated railway system, the regiment arrived in the North Korean capital Pyongyang soon after the Chinese

3

intervention in the conflict. A disorganized, head-long retreat then ensued as the United Nations Forces withdrew from North Korea to form a line below the 38th Parallel.

Throughout the bitter winter of 1950/51 the 8th Hussars were to learn the rigours of operating tanks in sub-zero temperatures, the lowest recorded being −16°F. At night the Centurions were parked on bundles of rice straw to prevent the tracks from freezing to the ground. Failure to do this would result in the total immobilisation of the tank and a burnt-out clutch as it struggled to extricate itself. In such extreme temperatures towing hawsers and draw-bars snapped, lubricants solidified; petrol stoppages were common as water droplets in the fuel lines froze them solid. The tanks had to be started up every hour or so, and each gear had to be engaged in turn to prevent freezing of control linkages and main components. The auxiliary charging engine was in constant use

in a vain attempt to heat the fighting compartment. Batteries cracked in the intense cold and had to be kept at a higher specific gravity to retain their charge. It was dangerous to touch the side of a tank with bare hands as the flesh would adhere to metal.

Even so, the Centurions performed well and mechanical problems were few. The crews suffered more from the cold than the tanks.

It was at the battle of the Imjin River in April 1951 that the Centurions of the 8th Hussars won lasting fame. They covered the withdrawal of 29th Brigade in heroic fashion in face of the overwhelming Chinese spring offensive. In October the 8th Hussars, now acting as the Armoured Regiment of 1st British Commonwealth Division, took part in Operation 'Commando', which was intended to advance the United Nations line across the Imjin River into the hills to the north, and to deny to the Communists positions they had prepared for a winter offensive. The terrain was appalling even by Korean standards and the Centurions were severely tested. Tracks shed as they attempted to scale impossible hills, and a number of tanks were lost to mines or 'bogging' in the paddy fields. Despite these difficulties, several

Following the Chinese intervention in the Korean War, the United Nations Forces were forced to retreat precipitously. Centurions Mk.3 of 'C' Sqn. 8th King's Royal Irish Hussars withdraw southwards along freezing, treacherous roads. The callsign plate on the turret rear of the leading Centurion signifies 4 Troop Leader of 'C' Sqn. (Soldier)

Centurions reached their objectives on high features from where they dominated the surrounding terrain, pounding Chinese positions with highly accurate 20pdr. fire and supporting infantry attacks with their co-axial Besas. The Centurions' ability to climb precipitous heights and the unmatched accuracy of their main armament won universal praise. This in turn led to many sales of Centurions to foreign armies. In a tribute to the 8th KRIH on their departure from Korea Major-General John O'Daniel, commanding First Corps, said: 'In their Centurions, the 8th Hussars have evolved a new type of tank warfare. They taught us that anywhere a tank can go is tank country – even the tops of mountains. . . .'

By the time the regiment was relieved by the 5th Royal Inniskilling Dragoon Guards in December 1951 the campaign had become static, and operations were reminiscent of the trench warfare in France from 1915 to 1918. The Centurions were dug-in among infantry company localities on the tops of hills. The tanks were protected from shellfire by sandbags and earth-filled ammunition containers. Crews lived beside their tanks at first in tents but later, as enemy artillery fire increased, in dug-outs or 'hutchies' carved out of the hillsides. There was no movement of tanks except when squadrons were relieved or for occasional maintenance when vehicles were withdrawn below the skyline. In the mountainous country, both sides held commanding features on the high ground with the intervening valley floor as 'No Man's Land.'

During the day, tank crews kept constant watch through binoculars for signs of enemy activity. Any fresh diggings, bunkers or trenches were quickly engaged by 20pdr. HE. Within a short time the crews knew the dispositions of all enemy earthworks and the exact range to each of them. Any enemy unwise enough to show himself during daylight was liable to suffer a volley of 20pdr. rounds within seconds. Even in the grim desolation of Korea there were lighter incidents, such as the Chinese soldier who every morning trod the same path to his hillside latrine. Every morning he was saluted with a near miss. This invariably produced a friendly wave in return.

By night the tale was very different. Both sides patrolled aggressively in 'No Man's Land' up to

'Caughoo', Centurion Mk.3 of 'C' Sqn. HQ Troop, fired the first rounds in action in support of an American infantry patrol along the banks of the Han river, 11 February 1951. After a short but decisive engagement against a captured Cromwell tank, the Centurion continued its accurate fire support against enemy POL supplies hidden behind the Cromwell. (Soldier)

the opposing lines. Ambushes were set and limited raids undertaken. In all cases the tanks acted as fire support, engaging pre-selected targets as dictated by the infantry. Prior to an infantry patrol the tanks would register on likely troublespots and potential ambush sites. The range, azimuth and angle of declination were established by daylight during normal harassing shoots and recorded for later reference. Each scheduled target had a code name or number, and it took only seconds for a

Centurion Mk.3 of 'B' Sqn. 8 KRIH fires on enemy positions during Operation 'Commando', the first operation conducted by 1st British Commonwealth Division after the amalgamation of all Commonwealth units in July 1951. Typical of the fighting in Korea, the Centurion is perched on a commanding hilltop from where the accurate, direct fire of the 20 pdr. dominated the surrounding terrain. (Australian War Memorial)

During the static phase of the Korean War tanks were emplaced in hulldown positions among the entrenched infantry companies. A Centurion Mk.3 of 1 RTR sits on the right hand half-troop position of Point 159. To either side of the tank ammunition bunkers were dug into the hillside with the crew's 'hutchie' to the right. Point 159 was overlooked on three sides by Communist positions and was subjected to continual harassing fire, stripping the hill of all vegetation and pulverising the ground around the tank. (Colonel Peter Massey)

tank to execute the fire plan on command from an infantry patrol in 'No Man's Land'. Against massed enemy infantry attacks, which invariably occurred at night, the supporting fire of tanks was an important adjunct to Divisional artillery. Several Centurions were fitted with American searchlights over the main armament in order to illuminate enemy patrols in 'No Man's Land'. Tanks normally worked in pairs, one to bathe the suspected area in light while the other engaged the target with HE. The searchlights were vulnerable to small arms fire and artillery fragments, however, and required the main engine to be run at almost peak revs to produce sufficient electrical power.

A number of limited armoured raids were conducted by the 'Skins' during 1952. Although these were generally successful, the unfavourable terrain and risk of losing tanks to 'bogging' and mines, which would result in extensive and protracted recovery operations, cast doubts on their value and they were discontinued. The Chinese held no doubts as to the efficiency of the Centurions and attempted to force their withdrawal from the hilltops. For five days in May 1952 a concentrated artillery assault fell on the tanks. The Centurions received 45 direct hits during that time. No crews secure inside their Centurions were injured and little damage was incurred beyond smashed peri-

scopes, radio aerials, bazooka plates and stowage bins. Two tanks had to be evacuated but were quickly replaced. The enemy did not succeed in his object, but such was the discomfort of the surrounding infantry under the heavy shellfire that some tanks were withdrawn below the skyline by day and only moved up to their fire positions at night.

Dismayed by their lack of success against the tanks, the Chinese continued to harass them with artillery and mortars. An apocryphal story relates that they offered 'one million pounds for a Centurion tank and 7/6d [37½p] for the head of Major Garnett' (a 'Skins' officer of 'B' Sqn.).

In the peculiar circumstances of Korea even a single tank was often a decisive factor. On the night of 18/19 November 1952, 4 Troop, 'B' Sqn. under Lt. M. Anstice was in support of 1st Bn., The Black Watch entrenched on an important hill feature known as the Hook which abutted directly on to the Chinese positions. At 2100 hrs. a heavy artillery bombardment fell on the hill, followed by massed waves of Chinese infantry. The tank troop was deployed in two groups at either end of the feature assisted by a fifth tank to the east on a hill called Yong Dong. Using their searchlights the Centurions opened fire on the enemy forming-up positions (FUP) and axes of advance. The searchlights were effective in illuminating targets until masked by the smoke of battle or knocked out by enemy fire. The Chinese overran the forward platoon of 'A' Company 1st Black Watch, who withdrew into their bunkers, directing the divisional artillery on to their own positions. By 2225 hrs. the weight of artillery defensive fire and the supporting fire of the tanks had driven the enemy back. The Centurions had been hit repeatedly, searchlights destroyed, trackguards and stowage bins shot away. The fumes inside the tanks were appalling as their extractor fans were unable to cope with the concentrated firing of both main and co-axial armaments. The loader/operator in the troop leader's tank was overcome by fumes and was replaced when the tanks withdrew to replenish with ammunition.

A second Chinese attack followed at midnight, and once again the Hook was occupied. At this juncture the commanding officer of 1st Black Watch asked for a tank to climb on to the Hook to support a counter-attack by 'B' Company. At first the troop leader demurred at this somewhat impractical suggestion but duly complied, and Centurion 'Black Bob' (callsign 4) set off up the narrow twisting track shrouded in smoke. Halfway up the hill the Centurion was obstructed by two Royal Artillery vehicles parked outside the Gunner's OP bunker. Reporting the obstacle, Lt. Anstice was ordered to proceed. In first gear the Centurion slowly climbed over the abandoned vehicles crushing them in a screech of grinding metal. At the top of the hill 'Black Bob' moved forward firing its Besa, but was immediately struck on the glacis plate by a 3.5 inch bazooka rocket. Trooper Lewis, the driver, was badly wounded and the tank caught fire. Enemy machine guns opened up on the tank, on fire and silhouetted against the night sky by a searchlight from Yong Dong. Lance-Corporal Williamson, the replacement loader/operator, leapt from the turret and extinguished the fire around the mantlet cover and stowage bins. Tpr. Lewis was pulled through

into the turret and L/Cpl. Williamson scrambled into the driving compartment. Donning the blood-wet headphones, he skillfully drove the Centurion back down the hill while the tank on Yong Dong illuminated the track with its searchlight. After Tpr. Lewis was evacuated the tank resumed its fire support rôle.

At 0200 hrs., a counter-attack by 'A' Company 1st Black Watch retook the Hook. The final Chinese assault came at 0450 hrs., but at first light a counter-attack by 'C' Company, 1st Bn., Princess Patricia's Canadian Light Infantry finally cleared the Hook. At 0940 hrs. 4 Troop, 'B' Sqn. withdrew to their harbour positions after nine

Australian troops of 3 RAR inspect a Centurion Mk.3 of 'B' Sqn. 1 RTR in a typical hilltop position. The tank mounts an 18in. General Electric searchlight over the main armament. A number of Centurions in Korea carried such devices to illuminate enemy patrols in 'No Man's Land' at night. Tank name is 'Fuka' after the North African battle of the Second World War. The 'B' Sqn. insignia of a red square with white outline is just visible below the smoke grenade launchers and on the rear hull plate. Smoke from the engine decks indicates the auxiliary charging set engine is in use to provide electrical power for turret traverse and gun control equipment. (Australian War Memorial)

The remains of the Royal Artillery Willys Jeep and 15cwt truck after being crushed by the Centurion Mk.3 of Lt. M. Anstice, 4 Troop 'B' Sqn. 5th Royal Inniskilling Dragoon Guards, during the second battle of the Hook, 18 November 1952. (5RIDG)

Tpr. Wells, the gunner of 'Black Bob', holds aloft a 3.5in. bazooka rocket found on the day after the Hook battle in which the tank was pierced by bazooka, wounding the driver. The penetration hole can be seen in the glacis plate just below the driver's hatch beside Tpr. Wells. The hole was repaired by inserting a track pin, cut to length and then welded into position. (Peter Williamson)

hours of close engagement with the enemy. Lt. Anstice was awarded the Military Cross for his gallantry in the battle.

In December 1952, 1st Royal Tank Regiment replaced the 'Skins'. 1 RTR continued the task of harassing the enemy and dominating 'No Man's Land' by day. At night they fired pre-registered DFs to the front of infantry positions to counter enemy attacks and in support of friendly patrols. Infantry raids to capture prisoners and destroy tunnels were also supported by tank fire. An interesting technique of night fighting was evolved whereby infantry using infra-red obser-vation devices tracked enemy patrols until they passed certain pre-registered points, when the tanks engaged them with HE.

The Chinese mounted another fierce attack against the Hook in May 1953. The position was now held by 1st Bn., The Duke of Wellington's Regiment with 'C' Sqn., 1 RTR tanks in support. Throughout the action the Centurions engaged the enemy and inflicted heavy losses, firing 504 rounds of 20pdr. HE and 22,500 rounds of Besa. The tanks themselves suffered on average five direct hits each from shells and mortars, without loss.

On the occasion of the coronation of Her Majesty Queen Elizabeth II in June the guns of the Divisional artillery fired a *feu de joie* of red, white and blue smoke on to Chinese positions. As the smoke began to clear, all Centurions in the line each fired one round in a crashing salvo at a pre-selected target. In the following month 'C' Sqn. supported 1st US Marine Division to the left of the Hook as the Chinese recklessly sacrificed hundreds of soldiers in a final, futile attempt to capture the position. On 27 July 1953 a truce was signed at Panmunjon, and hostilities ceased.

A rare view of a Centurion ARV Mk.1 in action. Equipped with a rear-mounted jib, this ARV Mk.1 of 'C' Sqn. 1 RTR in Gloster Valley lifts the Merritt-Brown Z51R gearbox of a Centurion Mk.3. (Alan Campbell)

Operation 'Musketeer'—
Suez 1956

On 26 July 1956 Colonel Gamil Abdul Nasser proclaimed the nationalisation of the Suez Canal. Within days of the announcement the French and British governments decided on a joint military intervention to restore control of the international waterway. Three regiments of the Royal Armoured Corps were mobilised to meet the emergency. 1st and 6th Royal Tank Regiments were to provide armoured support to the assault forces, while 7th Royal Tank Regiment equipped with unarmoured LVTs Mk.3 was to land 40 and 42 Royal Marine Commandos over the beaches. Both 1 and 6 RTR were considerably under strength. Throughout August equipment and vehicles, many of them lacking such essential fittings as wireless sets and ammunition racks, were drawn from the length and breadth of England.

As the stipulated assault regiment, 1 RTR received first priority in equipment and training facilities while 6 RTR accepted what meagre resources remained. 6 RTR were able to achieve only one day of troop training on Salisbury Plain before both regiments were loaded on tank transporters for the journey to the embarkation ports of

In the rising tide of nationalism of the 1950s the British Army was increasingly employed on counter-insurgency operations. Few of these warranted the use of tracked vehicles, but when the vital water filtration plant which served the massive British Army camp at Shandur in the Suez Canal Zone was threatened by saboteurs and snipers sheltering in the nearby village of Kafr Abdu the Centurions of 10 Troop 4 RTR undertook Operation 'Flatten'. In December 1951 tanks demolished a number of houses harbouring snipers' nests which had fired on supply convoys plying between the water plant and Shandur. Note the RTR regimental crest within the 'C' Sqn. insignia of this Centurion Mk.3, and damage to trackguards, stowage bins and front roadwheel sustained during this unusual task for a battle tank. (Soldier)

Plymouth and Portland. Due to the lack of RASC drivers and insufficient tank transporters, many of the Centurions were carried by civilian contractors. Working strict union hours, the drivers of British Road Services and Pickfords displayed a distinctly casual and dilatory attitude to the whole affair; on one occasion a Centurion, fully stowed with ammunition and machine guns, was parked unattended in a roadside lay-by for a whole weekend while the lorry-driver retired to the local hostelry.

Considerable delay and confusion arose at the ports. Due to conflicting movement orders 6 RTR set sail first for Malta with 45 Centurions Mk.5 aboard the naval LSTs HMS *Suvla*, *Salerno*, *Ravager* and *Puncher*. On arrival the tanks were quartered on the Marsa Club No. 2 Polo pitch, much to the dismay of the expatriate sporting fraternity, who saw their playing field disintegrate

9

Dawn, 6 November 1956: an LCT carrying elements of 'C' Sqn. 6 RTR approaches the beaches of Port Said at the outset of the assault landings. The Centurions Mk.5 are fitted with metal trunking wading kits. Of particular interest, the leading Centurion tows two one-ton trailers carrying spare 20 pdr. rounds and ammunition as replenishment for the Royal Marine Commandos who landed first. (James Haddon)

under the tracks of the Centurions. After long weeks of intensive training and growing frustration the invasion force was called to readiness on 27 October and Operation 'Musketeer' finally got under way.

At 0415 hrs. on Tuesday 6 November the LCAs and LVT Buffalos of 7 RTR carrying 40 and 42 RM Commandos formed up and churned towards the shore while air strikes and naval gunfire pounded the beaches at Port Said. Behind them came the LCTs carrying the Centurions of 'C' Sqn., 6 RTR. Against a pall of black smoke from burning storage tanks the LCTs gently beached 150 yards offshore and the Centurions rumbled down the ramps into six feet of water. As the tanks rolled ashore the explosive charges retaining the waterproofing equipment were detonated. Unfortunately short circuits and corrosion of the explosive securing bolts after practice landings in Malta prevented the removal of exhaust and air intake stacks from six of the 14 tanks and the crews were obliged to dismantle the wading kits with crowbars and sledge hammers under sporadic Egyptian small arms fire, much to the amusement of Marines sheltering in the lee of the Centurions.

Within minutes of landing the tanks repelled an Egyptian counter-attack; and after securing the beachhead 9 and 10 Troops together with the OC of 'C' Sqn., Major John Joly, advanced into the town with the Commando LVTs. Moving at speed, the column came under heavy small arms fire from the side alleys and buildings lining the main street, Sharia Mohammed Ali. The Royal Marines in their unarmoured LVTs suffered several casualties. Unable to elevate their co-axial machine guns sufficiently, the tanks were prevented from returning the fire to the enemy in the upper storeys and the lack of cupola mounted Brownings was sorely felt. The crews of three 57mm anti-tank guns impeding the advance near the Egyptian Police Club were killed by the stabilised Brownings of the leading Centurions of 9 Troop under Sgt. Lumsden. Once out of the town the tanks formed defensive positions covering the Golf Course and dock areas, preventing the arrival of enemy reinforcements from the south until they were relieved by 'B' Sqn. during the afternoon.

On the other flank, 40 Commando with 11 Troop in support were clearing the waterfront and dock basins, but their rate of progress was necessarily slow. Each building had to be systematically searched and secured, while the maze of side streets afforded the enemy numerous avenues of infiltration and escape. By 0730 hrs. the Marines had advanced some 1,000 yards to the area of the Commercial Basin. Suddenly two Coca Cola trucks loaded with enemy infantry charged round a corner into the path of 11 Troop. The first was completely destroyed by a 20pdr. HE round at 200 yards; the other, riddled by Browning fire, careered out of control into the canal. An hour later, with the capture of the Canal Company offices, 40 Commando came under heavy fire from Navy House across the Arsenal Basin and the advance faltered due to lack of infantry. The gates of the Arsenal Docks leading to Navy House were demolished by the Centurion belonging to 11 Troop commander, 2nd Lt. H. Leach, and a timber yard concealing ammunition was set ablaze. Even so, fierce fighting continued and the stubborn resistance from Navy House was not finally subdued until mid-afternoon, when a Fleet Air Arm strike with rockets and cannon ignited the building.

While the battle raged in the streets a Centurion and section of Marines had been despatched to relieve the British Consulate, where the staff was held under house arrest. The mission was successful and the tank crew was suitably rewarded with tea served through the window by the Consul's butler. The Consul, his wife and their pet spaniel were then evacuated in a Saracen ambulance. At the same time 12 Troop, with the commanding officer of the Royal Marines, Brigadier Madoc, approached the Italian Consulate, where the Egyptian Military Governor was sheltering. The barred and shuttered doors proved an impediment to ceasefire negotiations, so the troop leader, Capt. Tim Green, drove his Centurion up the steps of the portico into the hall, whereupon the Egyptian commander volunteered to accompany Madoc to Brigade HQ.

By 0900 hrs., the LSTs *Ravager*, *Puncher* and *Salerno* carrying 'A' and 'B' Sqns. and Regimental HQ had docked beside the Casino Palace Hotel and the tanks were disembarked. Severe congestion in the beach-head delayed their progress. It took an hour and a half for 3 and 4 Troops and 'A' Sqn. HQ to negotiate the crowded streets along the waterfront, past the railway station to the Golf Course. As the tanks crossed the railway line the leading Centurion, '4 Alpha', was strafed with cannon by a 'friendly' aircraft. Fortunately little damage was incurred beyond a 20mm shell

embedded in the hull and the wrath of the tank commander, Sgt. Jacknik. Further misfortune struck almost immediately as the tracks broke through the crust into the slime beneath. Within minutes four Centurions were bogged and as the Squadron ARV was delayed in the town as a result of the fighting around the Arsenal Basin, the tanks were stranded. Meanwhile, 6 and 7 Troops of 'B' Sqn. under Major J. Allen were involved in fierce street fighting in the area of El Abbasi Mosque in Sharia El Mahrusa and the Arab Town in support of 42 and 45 Commandos. 5 and 8 Troops under Capt. C. Prateley set off to the Gas Works to relieve 9 and 10 Troops of 'C' Sqn., who were in desperate need of replenishment.

It was not until 1345 hrs. that the bogged tanks of 'A' Sqn. were recovered. Shortly afterwards the advance was resumed down the canal roads, with the support of redoubtable French Foreign Legion parachutists crouching on the backs of the Centurions. As darkness fell the force reached the

Centurion Mk.5 of 'B' Sqn. 6 RTR enters Port Said, where the squadron provided armour support to 42 and 45 RM Commandos operating in the Arab Town. Around the turret is the black stripe carried by all British and French tanks as a mutual recognition device. (ECP Armées)

canal station of El Tina and the infantry dug in while the tanks refuelled. Here they were joined by Lt.Col. T. Gibbon and his Regimental HQ at 2100 hrs. By now rumours of an impending ceasefire were rife and the Force Commander, Gen. Stockwell, ordered the advance to continue as far south as possible. Using captured Egyptian lorries and all available transport, 2 Parachute Battalion reached El Tina at 2300 hrs., where the two leading companies clambered aboard the Centurions. Driving without lights, the column motored at top speed down both canal roads and covered seven miles in 45 minutes, stopping to clear the canal stations of El Tina and El Cap on the way before halting at midnight some 1,500 yards south of El Cap when the ceasefire was declared.

L-Day + 1 dawned bright and clear with the regiment busily engaged in much needed maintenance and replenishment. At El Cap the monotony of the afternoon was broken by the incident that became known as the 'War of Jacknik's Ear'. Sgt. Jacknik was in the turret of the point tank, '4 Alpha', helping his operator Trooper Clark repair the wireless set, while Corporal Charlton, the driver, was preparing a meal on the canal side. Beside him the gunner, Tpr. Harty, cleaned the .30cal. Browning machine gun. Some 100 yards behind, the crew of Centurion '3 Alpha' observed a party of 25 armed Egyptians moving cautiously along Treaty Road from the south. Despite frantic

Centurions Mk.5 of 'A' Sqn. 6 RTR advance out of the town towards the Canal roads. The air recognition sign on the turret roof is easily visible on these vehicles. (ECP Armées)

endeavours to attract their attention the crew of '4 Alpha' remained oblivious of the enemy's approach until the patrol was almost parallel to the tank. Hearing voices, Sgt. Jacknik put his head out of the turret. The patrol leader shouted 'Hands up', only to receive a short Anglo-Saxon expletive in return, whereupon the patrol opened fire, a bullet nicking Sgt. Jacknik's ear. Dropping into the turret, he returned fire with a Sten gun while Sgt. Stebbings in '3 Alpha' fired one round of 20pdr. HE and a burst of Browning, killing two Egyptians and wounding others. These were the last shots fired by the Centurions of 6 RTR during Operation 'Musketeer'.

The Indo-Pakistani War of 1965

Since partition in 1947 friction between India and Pakistan over the disputed state of Jammu and Kashmir had been the cause of numerous incidents along the length of the border. In the summer of 1965, after a fierce three-week clash in the barren, uninhabited saltflats of the Rann of Kutch at the southernmost end of the frontier, Pakistan began a campaign of infiltration of Kashmir by armed irregular 'freedom fighters', with the object of fomenting insurrection among the predominantly Muslim population. In response, Indian infantry units crossed the ceasefire line on 24 August and seized two strategic hills in the area of Tithwal. Subsequently, the large salient opposite Srinagar was occupied: an area of approximately 250 square miles containing the important Haji Pir Pass, which was an alleged infiltration route of 'freedom fighters' from Pakistan. Open hostilities erupted on 1 September when Pakistan launched Operation 'Grand Slam' against the Chamb-Akhnur sector with two armoured regiments and an infantry brigade.

The initial Pakistani assault forced the two infantry battalions and a squadron of tanks defending the area to withdraw, but on account of unfavourable terrain and a lack of logistical support the attack faltered a few miles short of Akhnur, having gained approximately 190 square miles of Indian territory. The object of the operation was twofold: firstly, to occupy territory as a bargaining counter to the captured salient, and secondly to tempt the Centurions of the powerful Indian 1st Armoured Division from the Jammu area to the northern side of the River Chenab, where they would be forced to join battle with their backs to the fast-flowing, mile-wide river. The Indians did not rise to the bait, however, having no intention of committing their armour to such poor tank country, but instead decided to relieve the pressure by a counter-attack in strength further south towards Lahore in the Amritsar-Ferozepore area of Southern Punjab.

On 6 September five columns, each approximately of brigade strength amounting to three infantry divisions with an independent armoured brigade in support, launched simultaneous attacks into Pakistani territory. The area was not ideal for armour as the soft low-lying ground was crisscrossed by irrigation ditches and small rivers; but the advance made rapid progress until it reached

Centurion Mk.7 of the Indian 16th Independent Armoured Brigade advancing in a cloud of dust during the Indo-Pakistani War of 1971. No modifications were made to Centurions in Indian service. (Indian Army)

the main Pakistani defensive line of concrete pillboxes and gun emplacements on the Ichogil Canal. The canal was approximately 120 feet wide and 15 feet deep, forming a natural anti-tank obstacle, and despite some minor probes across it the Indian advance was contained.

On 7 September the Pakistanis counter-attacked in the Kasur area overunning the forward Indian infantry positions and forcing a withdrawal until the attack was halted by artillery fire. On the night of 8 September the Pakistani 1st Armoured Division of 4th and 5th Armoured Brigades, with a supporting infantry division, opened a major offensive employing M47 and M48 Pattons fitted with infra-red equipment to shell Indian positions. The Indian tanks lacked such facilities for night fighting. During the next day and a half the Pakistanis launched five sepa-

rate attacks culminating on the 10th in one of the most decisive armoured engagements of the war at the battle of Assal Uttar, a small village near the market town of Khem Karan.

Indian armour and infantry fell back in face of the repeated attacks, luring the Pakistanis into a large horseshoe-shaped trap near the village. On the morning of 10 September the Pakistanis committed the main strength of their armoured division with infantry in support. As they manoeuvred to outflank the Indian positions the tanks were hampered by the marshy conditions created when the Indians breached irrigation ditches and dykes. Spearheaded by M47 and M48 Pattons and flanked by M24 Chaffees and Shermans, the tank columns outstripped their lorry-borne infantry and were channelled into fields of tall-standing sugar cane, behind which the Indian tanks, including the Centurions of 3rd Cavalry, waited in hull-down positions. The high cane fields obscured visibility for the attackers, while the Indian tank gunners were able to track the Pattons

Pakistani M48 in the 'Patton-nagar' at Assal Uttar, victim of the 'three-round battle range technique' employed by Indian Centurions during the 1965 war. The third round was probably 'plus' of the target. (Indian Army)

by observing the waving sugar cane. Aiming a few feet below the exposed .50cal. machine guns atop the turrets of the Pattons, the Centurions opened fire, exacting a deadly toll even before the surviving Pakistani tanks broached the cane fields into the open to become victims of the Centurions on their flanks. The trap was closed by the supporting fire of 76mm-armed Shermans and jeep-mounted 106mm recoilless rifles. A total of 97 tanks were destroyed or captured in the battle of Assal Uttar in what became known as the 'Patton-nagar' – 'the Patton graveyard'.

Meanwhile, the fighting on the Sialkot front farther north had developed into the largest tank battle since the Second World War. On 8 September India mounted her main offensive from the Jammu area employing the 1st Armoured Division, equipped with three regiments of Centurions (Poona Horse, Hodson's Horse and 16th Cavalry), and two infantry divisions. Although the terrain was more suitable for armour than had been the case in the 'Patton-nagar' battle, the Indian tanks still outpaced their supporting infantry and clashed with the Pakistani 6th Armoured Division, which had similarly outrun its infantry. Over the next 15 days of almost continuous armoured action the two armies fought a bitter battle of attrition. A brief pause followed the initial clash. Fierce fighting then erupted in a series of armoured engagements known as the battle of Phillora, in which each side attempted to split the opposing forces and destroy them piecemeal. After the capture of Phillora by the Indians on the 12th both sides regrouped, reinforcing their armoured units from the Lahore sector and elsewhere. From the 14th to 17th there followed the battle of Chawinda, where tanks were committed to destroying tanks, both sides suffering heavy casualties. After this battle the fighting lost its ferocity but continued throughout the Sialkot sector until the ceasefire on 23 September.

These battles constituted the principal and most significant operations of the war. Both sides claimed victory in the conflict, but militarily it was a draw, with the Indians demonstrating greater tactical skill in the use of armour due to superior crew training. It must be realised that the Indian Armoured Corps had been seduced by Pakistani propaganda and entered the conflict in

A tank crew of 3rd Cavalry proudly display some of the 15 hits that their Centurion Mk.7 suffered in battle on the Lahore front, yet it remained operational. (Indian Army)

considerable trepidation, believing the Patton to be vastly superior in terms of firepower, protection and mobility to any tank possessed by the Indians. This concern was reflected in many of the official citations for heroism following the war, one of which commended an NCO for an action against 'several of the supposedly invulnerable Pattons...' Indeed, it appears the Pakistanis were victims of their own propaganda and believed the Patton to be virtually indestructible. This led to their rash tactics in assaulting Indian positions frontally and suffering proportionately higher losses among the Pattons, which invariably led their attacks. In the swirling dust of the Sialkot battles, Centurion fought Patton at ranges seldom exceeding 1,000 yards. The robust Centurion with its simpler fire control system proved superior to the M47 and M48 Pattons equipped with stereoscopic range-finders and sophisticated ballistic computers, which proved too complex for the ordinary Pakistani 'sowar'.

Throughout the conflict the Indian Centurions employed the 'battle range technique' of fire engagement with telling effect. The 'three-round battle range technique' was a simple and rapid method of tank gunnery devised by Col. Eric Offord during the 1950s when commandant of the RAC Gunnery Wing at Lulworth. In practice, the tank commander estimated whether the range to target was less than 1,000 yards. If so he gave the fire order – 'Sabot action!' The loader loaded an APDS round, while the gunner took his initial point of aim on the target with 800 yards on the APDS range scale, and fired the main armament. Irrespective of whether the target was hit (and in all probability observation of the result would be impossible due to obscuration), the gunner automatically took a point of lay at 1,000 yards, shouting 'Add 200, firing now!', and fired again. Without pausing, he took a point of aim at 600 yards, crying 'Drop 400, firing now!' and fired the main armament yet again. On account of the flat trajectory of the APDS round this ensured a hit at all ranges up to 1,000 yards and the three rounds were fired in under 20 seconds – often before the Pattons had fired their first shot.

As a result of the heavy casualties they inflicted the confidence of Indian tank crews soared. When the Centurion proved able to absorb extensive battle damage and still remain operational, it rose still further. A tank commander of 3rd Cavalry recalls how his Centurion rocked back on its suspension as if in recoil. Kicking his gunner in the back, he demanded to know why the main armament had been fired without permission, only to discover that the tank had been struck on the mantlet by a 90mm APCBC round at a range of approximately 1,000 yards which had failed to penetrate. Instances are known of Centurions surviving hits by HEAT projectiles, both 90mm and Cobra anti-tank guided missiles, with no more than the loss of a stowage bin or bazooka plate.

Although no longer in service today, the Centurion was held in the highest esteem by the Indian Armoured Corps. At the time it was being superseded by the Vijayanta many units wished to retain their Centurions in preference to the newer and lighter main battle tank.

The Six-Day War

Throughout the Six-Day War Centurions were at the forefront of the Israeli offensive in Sinai.[1] To the north Gen. Israel Tal's Division penetrated the Egyptian lines at Khan Yunis, and after a hard-fought battle at Rafah Junction, the Centurions of 7th Armoured Brigade broke through

heavily-fortified positions at Sheikh Zuweid and the Jiradi Pass, capturing El-Arish, capital of Sinai, by nightfall. Flanking this northern thrust, Gen. Abraham Yoffe's Division advanced across 30 miles of arid, trackless desert, hitherto thought impassable to tanks. Grinding through deep sand dunes, for much of the time in first gear, the leading battalion of Centurions blocked the Bir Larfan intersection, preventing Egyptian reinforcements from moving north to El-Arish.

On Tuesday 6 June Gen. Ariel Sharon captured the strategic position of Abu Agheila in a complex, set-piece battle. Employing his Centurions in a wide outflanking movement around the Egyptian emplacements, he struck at the enemy tanks from the rear. By 7 June the two principal Egyptian positions of Rafah and Abu Agheila had fallen and their armoured reserves had been severely mauled by the Centurions of Yoffe's Division.

The Egyptian Army began fleeing westwards. Their main line of retreat ran through a narrow defile 14 miles in length – the Mitla Pass. It was vital for the Israelis to seal the pass before the Egyptians could escape to the Suez Canal. The task fell to a Centurion battalion belonging to the Shadni Armoured Brigade of Yoffe's Division, composed entirely of reservists. In their race for the pass the Centurions were hampered by the columns of abandoned Egyptian vehicles blocking the road, many of them set ablaze by Israeli air strikes. Here and there Egyptian units fought on, delaying the advance and consuming precious fuel and ammunition. By the time the Centurions reached the Mitla Pass only nine tanks remained in the field. Two of these were being towed for lack of fuel. While deploying into fire positions three other Centurions ran out of petrol and had to be towed into a defensive formation. They were supported by two armoured infantry platoons and three half-tracks mounting 120mm mortars.

As dusk fell the retreating Egyptians reached the Mitla, and despite the blocking force an Egyptian column managed to bypass the Centurions and enter the pass. At that moment two Israeli Vautour bombers appeared overhead and dropped their bombs upon the congested vehicles causing a severe traffic jam. The Israeli commander realised he had to create his roadblock elsewhere and the diminutive force, towing their fuelless casualties,

[1] For further details of this and the 1948, 1956 and 1973 campaigns, see Vanguard 19, 'Armour of the Middle East Wars 1948–78'.

moved to within a mile of the Parker monument. There, in a bizarre incident, Centurion met Centurion in battle on opposing sides for the first time, the Egyptians having a few Centurions in the area. By tacit agreement, neither side fired on the other and the Egyptians withdrew.

The Israelis then pushed two Egyptian lorries across the road and set them on fire, obliging any retreating vehicle to decelerate and present an easy target for their Centurions' guns. Throughout the night the nine Centurions fought against an enemy many times their number. The critical fuel situation was alleviated somewhat by the arrival of an Israeli self-propelled artillery unit carrying 11 barrels of captured petrol. Having no filler funnels, the tank crews had to use empty biscuit tins. As each Centurion had a fuel capacity of 121 gallons it was a slow and back-breaking task. While they were refuelling, an Egyptian tank unit attempted to force the blockade. As the first T-54 passed the barricade of burning lorries one of them exploded in a ball of fire blinding the Israeli tank gunners. When the first T-54 was spotted again one Centurion commander mistakenly thought

Initially the Centurion was decidedly unpopular within the Israeli Armoured Corps, and detractors condemned it as being too complex – 'more suited to English garden lawns than to the dust of the Negev'. Centurion Mk.5 with 20 pdr. B Type barrel on manoeuvres in the Negev Desert prior to the Six-Day War. Originally an early production Mark 3, this Centurion was fitted with the .30 cal. Browning as a co-axial machine gun altering the vehicle to Mark 5. The driver wears a Russian tank crewman's padded helmet which proved much too hot for desert conditions. (Israeli Army)

his unit was advancing into the Mitla. He immediately followed the T-54, but on realising his error he fired an armour-piercing shell into the rear of the Egyptian tank at point-blank range. The Centurion them manoeuvred into a dominating fire position from where it could hit the rear of any tank penetrating the blockade.

In groups of 15 to 20 tanks the Egyptians tried repeatedly to break through the thin screen of Centurions. On one occasion 22 SU-100 self-propelled guns entered the pass; one managed to get through – the remainder were destroyed at ranges of 100–200 yards.

By dawn of 8 June the Israeli tanks were out of fuel again and critically low on ammunition. Only four Centurions were still mobile when a large

Centurion Mk.5 in the Sinai Desert at the outset of the Six-Day War. Typical of this period, the Centurions have .50 cal. M2HB Brownings at the commanders' cupolas, and the crews wear American tankers crash helmets with Uzi submachine guns as personal weapons. (Israeli Army)

additional 20 tons [sic] of armour steel. And the point which in my opinion shows more than anything else how we did it, were the stories about tanks which got five, six, seven hits – and there is one with 12 direct hits – and which continued to fight. But let me just tell of a few incidents. Two tanks which participated until half way through the battles, limping along on half of their chains. They were hit by a mine and damaged: they shortened their tracks and were able, at a slow pace, to continue in the fight. One tank was hit at the top by a direct 120mm [122mm] shell, and its turret became immobile. The officer in command decided to keep this tank at the rear, and so it advanced. At the battle of Gebel Jidi this tank is credited with hitting two enemy tanks.'

Vietnam 1968–1971

column of retreating Egyptians appeared including 28 T-54 tanks. Calling for air support, the four Centurions held the Egyptian tanks at bay until two Super-Mystères arrived to strafe and bomb the enemy column. From then on the Israeli Air Force destroyed the retreating convoys as they converged on the Mitla Pass. When the battle died down, burnt and abandoned Egyptian vehicles stretched for three miles before the pass. With little time for rest or re-organization the Centurions surged on towards the Suez Canal.

After the war, the brigade commander, Col. Iska Shadni, whose armoured battalion had fought this gallant action at the Mitla Pass, had some illuminating comments to make concerning the campaign and his Centurion tanks: 'When I ask myself how is it possible that against the might of the Egyptian Army, which my armoured columns had to face, continuously changing their positions, I was able to destroy 157 enemy tanks, while our losses were almost nil – well, how did that happen? I have to give the following explanations: First of all, I agree with what has been said by the others before [the superior training and tactical handling of the Israeli Army]. Second, the air force. Third, to my mind it was proved that the Centurion tank is by far superior to the T-55 and T-54 Russian tanks; and especially in one aspect – which gave our boys their self-confidence: the

In 1968, as part of Australia's increasing military commitment to the war, a tank squadron was deployed in support of 1st Australian Task Force in South Vietnam. The first elements of 'C' Sqn., 1st Armoured Regiment, comprising two troops of Centurions Mark 5/1 (Aust) with support vehicles, landed at Vung Tau in February. Critics in the Australian Parliament and elsewhere doubted the viability of tanks in tropical conditions where, they believed, the paddy fields and impenetrable jungle would limit their effectiveness to the rôle of static pillboxes. Despite this scepticism the Centurions proved a success in numerous rôles including fire support, perimeter defence, direct assault of enemy positions and, most importantly, infantry support. The infantry battalions were quick to appreciate the firepower of the Centurions as previously their only direct support had been from the .50cal. machine guns of M113A1s.

After an initial period of training in infantry co-operation the tanks participated in Operation 'Pinaroo' to invest the Long Hai hills, a Viet Cong safe haven of long standing, situated in the south of Phuoc Tuy Province. Acting in the fire support rôle, the Centurions engaged bunkers and cave-mouths while the rifle companies penetrated the enemy base areas. The pin-point accuracy of the 20pdr. main armament enabled infantry units to co-ordinate their assaults against enemy positions to a much higher degree than was possible with the close air support of helicopter gunships or ground-attack aircraft.

In May, during Allied operations to counter an enemy offensive against Saigon, the Centurions were a decisive factor in the successful perimeter defence of Fire Support Bases 'Coral' and 'Balmoral' against repeated North Vietnamese Army assaults. In conjunction with artillery and airpower, the canister fire of the Centurions decimated the attackers as they attempted to breach the perimeter wire. Discharging steel shards over a wide area at great velocity, canister is a cruel and devastating weapon against unprotected human beings. It also proved a most effective means of clearing the camouflage and vegetation which often concealed enemy bunker systems. Many engagements in Vietnam were fought against such systems, as the VC/NVA rarely initiated an action except from prepared positions. Often of great complexity and immense strength, the bunkers were all but invulnerable to artillery fire and infantry weapons. Without tank support the infantry were hard pressed to capture a position: but no bunker could withstand a pounding from APCBC solid shot at a few yards' range. Experience had shown that enemy bunkers, once taken, had to be destroyed to prevent later re-occupation. Demolition by explosives flown in by helicopters was time consuming and not always feasible. In such cases Centurions were usually able to accomplish the job simply by crushing the bunkers beneath their tracks.

With guidance from an airborne observer, the Centurions were able to negotiate most of Phuoc Tuy Province in the dry season. During the monsoons they were still able to reach almost every area where they were required. Beside the many rivers and watercourses, the greatest impediments to mobility were the jungle forests of tropical evergreen and bamboo. Progress through such terrain was extremely slow. An advance through thick bamboo would be measured in hundreds of yards per hour, while petrol consumption was often as high as 12 gallons to the mile. Clinging vines and falling trees damaged trackguards and stowage bins, necessitating frequent replacement. Exterior fittings such as headlight assemblies and smoke grenade dischargers were torn off entirely.

Centurion Mk.5/1 (Aust) of 2 Troop 'C' Sqn., 1st Armoured Regiment, at Fire Support Base 'Balmoral', Binh Duong Province, South Vietnam, May 1968. The Centurions were a major factor in the successful perimeter defence of FSB 'Balmoral' when an attacking NVA regiment was decimated by the canister fire of the tanks. (Australian War Memorial)

Similarly, despite fears of the enemy's effective RPG weapons, bazooka plates were soon discarded after arrival in Vietnam, as mud and vegetation compacted around the suspension units, distorting trackguards and stowage bins, which often lost their contents in the process. A remedy was found in replacing the original trackguards with steel plate of a thicker gauge. At the same time the stowage bins were reinforced and the bin-catches protected by welding mild steel angle along the sides. Spare roadwheels were fitted to the glacis plate, simplifying resupply and allowing speedy replacement after mine damage or an extended road run, when the high temperatures induced shedding of rubber tyres.

The enemy soon gained a healthy respect for Centurions' firepower and often withdrew from prepared ambush positions when an approaching infantry unit was accompanied by tanks. Deserters told of the terror felt by the enemy when opposed by Centurions. This fear was exploited by adopting a tactical manoeuvre known as 'the hammer and anvil'. The infantry would prepare ambushes on routes out of enemy occupied territory. The tanks would then sweep through the area. The enemy invariably fled on to the guns of the waiting infantry.

Yet, against an enemy as courageous and resourceful as that faced in Vietnam, Centurions did not fight without loss. Throughout the conflict the principal weapon employed against AFVs was the mine, accounting for almost 70 per cent of vehicle casualties. Against the Australians the VC/NVA used the standard ChiCom anti-tank mine, together with devices improvised from unexploded shells and bombs. Thanks to their external suspension units, Centurions survived ChiCom mines with relative impunity. Damage was usually restricted to a single suspension unit, which was readily replaced in the field with a spare flown in by Medium Lift Helicopter. The enemy soon realised the inadequacy of the ChiCom issue and constructed some monstrous mines from artillery

Centurions Mk.5/1 (Aust) of 'C' Sqn. 'scrub-bashing' through typical jungle growth during Operation 'Overlord', June 1971. 'Overlord' was one of the most successful examples of tank/infantry co-operation when Centurions of 'C' Sqn. gave decisive fire support to the infantry of 3rd Battalion Royal Australian Regiment against an NVA battalion strongly entrenched in an extensive bunker system in the north of Phuoc Tuy Province. (Australian War Memorial)

shells and explosives; yet, despite numerous attempts, only one Centurion was completely destroyed by such means. Several others were damaged beyond local repair, and these were returned to Australia to be renovated.

The other main anti-tank weapon in the enemy's armoury, the rocket-propelled grenade (RPG), proved only moderately successful. Despite their initial fears, tank crews were relieved to learn that the Centurion was capable of absorbing RPG hits to the suspension, hull and turret and often remained operational. Unless a crew member happened to be in the direct path of a penetration the damage was often slight, all the vulnerable ammunition being stowed below the level of the turret ring and protected by the external suspension units. The spare roadwheels on the glacis plate and the turret stowage bins were often sufficient to dissipate the effectiveness of the RPG. On 6 June 1969 an assault by Centurions of 3 Troop, 'B' Sqn. against an entrenched VC/NVA force occupying the village of Binh Ba was met

with a barrage of RPG rockets. In the ensuing action the tanks were hit numerous times, sustaining several crew casualties and appreciable damage; but they returned to the fray and, with the aid of infantry in M113A1 APCs, quelled the fierce resistance. One commander had a harrowing experience when ducking an RPG round: as it passed over his Centurion, his back was slashed by its fins.

Significantly, most casualties among tank crews were caused by rockets exploding above or on the outsides of the tanks. In the oppressive heat of the tropics tank crews rarely closed their hatches except in the direst circumstances. By firing RPGs into the trees above a tank or at the turret roof the enemy inflicted a number of serious casualties from the fragments and spall of an exploding rocket.

During Operation 'Hermit Park' in June 1971 a composite troop of 'C' Sqn. (on its second tour of duty) was given the task of destroying a strongly-held bunker system. As the tanks crashed through thick bamboo, the leading Centurion was struck twice by RPG rockets, destroying the cupola machine gun and seriously wounding the commander and wireless operator. Two other Centurions returned fire with canister and machine

Centurions Mk.5/1 (Aust) of 'A' Sqn. on Operation 'Matilda', January 1970, the largest Australian armoured operation since the Second World War. By 1970 the Centurions had been modified to meet the operational peculiarities of the Vietnamese theatre including reinforced trackguards and stowage bins and spare roadwheels on the glacis plate. Towing hawsers are draped around the glacis plate for speedy attachment during recovery operations in case of 'bogging'. The main armament and machine gun muzzles are masked with tape to prevent vegetation from fouling the barrels when operating in jungle. (Australian War Memorial)

guns; one of these was hit by RPG, wounding the gunner. The fourth Centurion took RPG hits in the suspension and gun barrel from a concealed weapons pit.

As the enemy infantryman raised his rocket launcher once again the Centurion fired its main armament and the position disintegrated under the impact of an APCBC shell, which incidentally ripped eight inches off the muzzle of the 20pdr. gun. The tank fired five more rounds of canister from its truncated gun, clearing the vegetation which covered the weapon pits; these were then silenced by machine gun fire.

Despite constant employment the ageing Centurions achieved a remarkable record of availability in Vietnam, rarely falling below 75 per cent. The devoted attention of tank crews and untiring dedication of RAEME LAD and workshops ensured that continual demands from infantry units for tank support were met. Operational track mileages were considerable and squadrons covered in excess of 50,000 miles in a 12-month period. As part of the reduction of Australian forces in Vietnam, the tank squadron was withdrawn from operations in August 1971 and returned to Australia in September. Those who had doubted the efficacy of armoured forces in jungle warfare were now staunch believers.

The October War 1973

The Golan Plateau is an area of undulating, treeless ground dotted with tall volcanic hills that dominate the surrounding terrain. It is poor tank country. In many places the lava fields and basalt outcrops are impassable to tanks, restricting their movement to roads and primitive tracks. Wheeled vehicles are unable to negotiate much of the plateau, it being especially punishing to vehicle suspensions. For this reason the Israelis employ predominantly Centurions on the Golan in preference to M48s and M6os, whose torsion bar suspension systems have proved less effective over the rock-strewn ground.

Along the 1967 border known to the Israelis as the 'Purple Line' 17 strongpoints had been constructed on the commanding heights. Each had a garrison of approximately 20 men supported by up to a platoon of tanks. An anti-tank ditch 15 feet wide by ten feet deep had been dug along the front from Mount Hermon in the north to the Yarmouk Valley on the Jordanian border. Large numbers of mines were laid only days before fighting began.

Approximately five miles to the rear of these static defences, the 'Barak' 188th Armoured Brigade, a component of Brig.Gen. Raful Eytan's 36th Division, was deployed as a mobile counter-attack force with approximately 70 Upgraded Centurions in three understrength battalions. One

An Upgraded Centurion speeds across the rock-strewn ground of the Golan to a new fire position while a hulldown Upgraded Centurion provides covering fire. Note the vehicle registration number is repeated on the barrel of the 105mm gun near the muzzle. (Israeli Army)

battalion was dispersed among the infantry strong-points. Just prior to the war 7th Armoured Brigade moved to the Golan and was deployed around Nafekh as divisional reserve. Equipped with three battalions of Upgraded Centurions, the 7th was one of the most distinguished regular units of the Israeli Defence Forces. It had fought in numerous actions on the Golan and its troops, commanded by Col. Avigdor 'Yanush' Ben Gal, were totally familiar with the terrain.

When fighting erupted on 6 October, the Israelis had two armoured brigades with 177 Centurions and one infantry brigade supported by 11 batteries of self-propelled artillery to defend the plateau. Arrayed against them were three Syrian infantry divisions, each of one infantry brigade, one mechanised brigade and one armoured brigade. Each division possessed 180 tanks, making a total of 540 tanks in the first assault. Behind them were poised the 1st and 3rd Armoured Divisions with 460 T-62 and T-55 tanks and a number of assorted independent armoured brigades. Approximately 1,300 Syrian tanks were crammed into the confines of the plateau. The infantry divisions were ordered to breach the Israeli defences with their tanks; then the armoured divisions would sweep through and recapture the Golan before the Israelis could mobilise their reserves. This achieved, the River Jordan and hills of Galilee would lie open to the Syrian Army.

The assault began at 1350 hrs. on Saturday 6

A platoon of Upgraded Centurions during a lull in the fighting. The photograph clearly shows the barren, undulating terrain of the Golan plateau. In the distance columns of black smoke billow from the burning wrecks of Syrian tanks. The accurate fire of Israeli tanks at long ranges led to Syrian accusations of them being equipped with laser rangefinders, but it was the tank crews' intimate knowledge of the terrain that was the decisive factor. (Israeli Army)

October, with air-strikes and intensive artillery fire against Israeli gun positions, tank parks and supply points. Tactical surprise was complete. Behind a creeping barrage, the Syrian divisions advanced through a curtain of dust on three major axes, one to the north of Kuneitra and two to the south. Moving in columns two abreast down either side of the roads the Syrian tanks struck the Israeli lines, bypassing the infantry strongpoints. Close to the front were specialist AFVs – mine-rollers, mine ploughs and bridging vehicles. The Centurions moved to their prepared fire positions; these were ramps situated on the numerous volcanic mounds which had been flattened by bull-dozers with the spoil heaped up to form hull-down positions. Opening fire at ranges of 2,000 yards or more, the Israelis concentrated on the specialist AFVs attempting to breach the anti-tank ditch.

By late afternoon Syrian pressure was mounting despite heavy losses. Brig. Eytan ordered Col. Ben Gal to despatch one of his tank battalions to reinforce the 'Barak' Brigade. 7th Armoured Brigade now took responsibility for the defence north of Kuneitra, absorbing the tank battalion from 'Barak' Brigade already in action there, a total force of approximately 50 Centurions. The third battalion of 7th Armoured Brigade remained in divisional reserve and was subsequently drawn into the fighting for the southern Golan.

The attack of the Syrian 7th Infantry Division north of Kuneitra was delayed at the anti-tank ditch by a lack of earth-moving and bridging equipment at the head of the columns. Some tanks did manage to cross into a valley between Mount Hermonit and a hill feature called 'Booster' by the Israelis. Behind the saddle connecting these two heights lay the Centurions of the 'Barak' battalion in prepared fire positions. By nightfall the valley was littered with burning Syrian hulks. Under the cover of darkness Syrian engineers levelled the ditch, their bright yellow Caterpillar D8 Dozers fleetingly visible amid the gunflashes and artillery flares. Aided by infra-red night-vision devices, the Syrian tanks advanced through the valley. The Centurions, which did not have such equipment, held their fire until the Syrian tanks were visible in the bright moonlight which reflected off the headlights and spotlights. For five hours the Centurions fired at the enemy muzzle flashes, aided by the light from burning wrecks. At 0300 hrs. on the 7th the Syrians withdrew to the ditch, leaving over 70 destroyed AFVs along the front of 7th Brigade.

Meanwhile, south of Kuneitra, the plight of the 'Barak' Brigade had become desperate. To cover a front of 25 miles with 70 tanks was almost impossible. The Syrian armour steadily outflanked the defending Centurions, whose arcs of fire were extended beyond the limits of their prepared ramp positions. The Centurions were forced to withdraw to ambush sites among the boulders and wadis. Here they continued the struggle, but without infantry support they were vulnerable to dismounted infantry RPG-7 teams. By midnight they had lost almost half their tanks. As dawn broke, collapse seemed inevitable. Then, during the morning, reinforcements began to appear. Irrespective of mobilisation plans and without waiting to form battalions or even companies, Centurions and Shermans were thrown into the battle on the southern Golan. Maj.Gen. Dan Laner, who took over the sector during the morning, had approximately 60 tanks under his command, including less than 20 remaining from the 'Barak' Brigade. Perched on the last high ground east of the Golan escarpment, these tanks fought back desperately against the tenacious attacks by the Syrian 5th Infantry and 1st Armoured Divisions.

In the northern sector 7th Armoured Brigade was still heavily engaged against the Syrian 7th and 9th Infantry Divisions. Two major attacks were repulsed during the morning, only to be followed by another ferocious assault in the afternoon. Almost 200 Syrian AFVs lay destroyed in the area between Hermonit and 'Booster'; the Israelis called it 'The Valley of Tears'. By now Col. Ben Gal had only two tank battalions and a small reserve left. His men were rapidly tiring and his tanks were desperately low on ammunition and fuel. Jeeps of his reconnaissance unit moved from tank to tank with rounds of 105mm ammunition salvaged from knocked-out Centurions. Israeli tank crews had been wasteful of rounds as a result of faulty selection of ammunition and target priorities, which often led to them firing on tanks that were already destroyed. In many cases this was deliberate since the Syrians had infiltrated artillery observers into knocked-out tanks, from where they brought down a fearsome fire on Israeli positions. So intense were the barrages that Israeli tank commanders, who habitually fought with their head and shoulders exposed to obtain better battle visibility, were now forced to close down. Even so the numbers of Israeli dead rose sharply, especially among tank commanders, many of whom were killed by turret-top fittings such as aerial bases and periscope heads, dislodged by the blast of exploding shells.

In support of 7th Armoured Brigade were the only batteries of M109 SP Guns the Israelis possessed. Although they were directed by field computer, their accurate salvoes of 155mm HE did little to deter the 'buttoned-up' Syrian tanks. Only White Phosphorus rounds proved effective; these burst open the vulnerable external fuel cells, despite the fact that the Syrians had covered them with sandbags for extra protection. Supplies of White Phosphorus were soon expended and once again it fell to the Centurions to halt the onslaught.

Throughout Sunday 7 October the Golan battle raged relentlessly. All reserve units were committed on arrival to the southern Golan where the risk of breakthrough was greatest. Then, at

MECHILE

1. Centurion Mark 1, 'B' Sqn., 1st Royal Tank Regt.;
   Detmold, Germany, 1947

2. Centurion Mark 3, HQ Troop, 'C' Sqn., 8th King's Royal Irish Hussars;
   Yongdungpo, Korea, February 1951 (Capt. G. Strachan MC)

CAUGHOO

FIRST AID BOX

41

A

ARROMANCHES

PEARL

1. Centurion Mark 3, 3 Tp., 'C' Sqn., 1st Royal Tank Regt.; The Hook, Korea, May 1953 (Sgt. A. Wallace MM)

2. Centurion ARV Mark 1, 'C' Sqn., 1st Royal Tank Regt.; Gloster Valley, Korea, 1953 (Sgt. T. George, RNZAC)

COMMONWEALTH

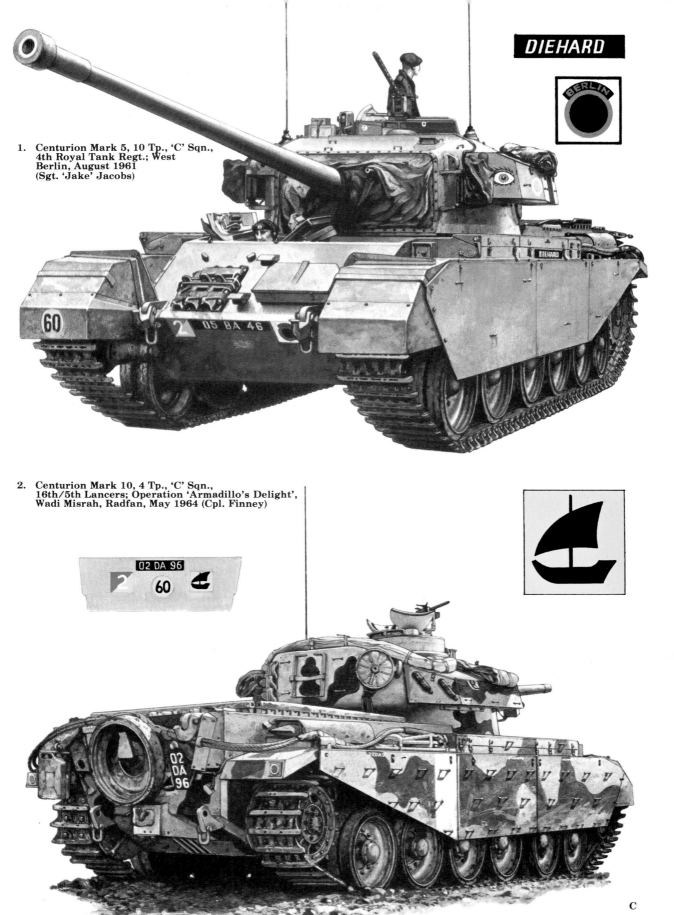

DIEHARD

1. Centurion Mark 5, 10 Tp., 'C' Sqn.,
   4th Royal Tank Regt.; West
   Berlin, August 1961
   (Sgt. 'Jake' Jacobs)

2. Centurion Mark 10, 4 Tp., 'C' Sqn.,
   16th/5th Lancers; Operation 'Armadillo's Delight',
   Wadi Misrah, Radfan, May 1964 (Cpl. Finney)

C

ANKUSH

1. Centurion Mark 7, Maj.Gen. Rajinder Singh,
GOC Indian 1st Armoured Division; North Punjab, September 1965

2. Centurion Mark 5, unit unknown, Israeli Defence Forces;
Sinai, June 1967

D

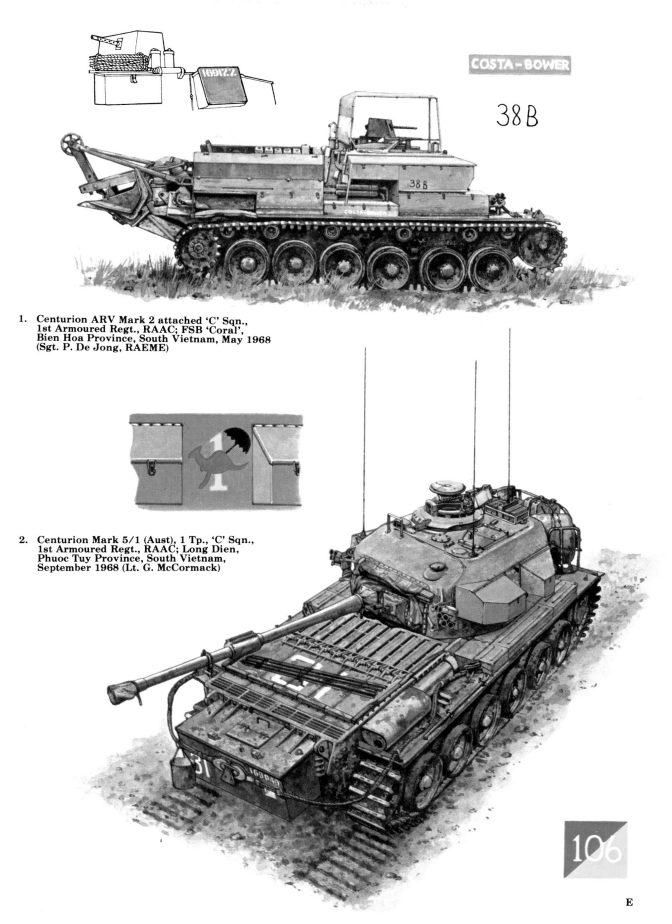

COSTA – BOWER

38B

1. Centurion ARV Mark 2 attached 'C' Sqn.,
1st Armoured Regt., RAAC; FSB 'Coral',
Bien Hoa Province, South Vietnam, May 1968
(Sgt. P. De Jong, RAEME)

2. Centurion Mark 5/1 (Aust), 1 Tp., 'C' Sqn.,
1st Armoured Regt., RAAC; Long Dien,
Phuoc Tuy Province, South Vietnam,
September 1968 (Lt. G. McCormack)

106

E

1. Centurion Mark 7, Jordanian 40th Armoured Bde.; battle of Ramtha, September 1970

2. Centurion AVRE, 26th Armd.Sqn. Royal Engineers; Operation 'Motorman', Londonderry, July 1972

1. Upgraded Centurion, Israeli 79th Armoured Bde.; Golan Heights, October 1973

2. Upgraded Centurion, Israeli Defence Forces; Operation 'Litani River', southern Lebanon, March 1978

G

1. Lieutenant, 1st Royal Tank Regt.; Korea, 1953

2. Sergeant, RAEME, 1st Royal Australian Armd. Regt.;
   South Vietnam, 1968

3. 1st Lieutenant and Private,
   Israeli Armoured Corps;
   Golan Heights, 1973

H

around 1500 hrs., the Syrian columns inexplicably ground to a halt. Their high command was disconcerted by their lack of success against 7th Armoured Brigade. All night they paused within sight of their objectives, while Israeli reservists poured on to the Golan. When they resumed their advance in the morning, momentum was irrevocably lost.

To the north the fighting between the Syrian 7th Infantry Division and the Israeli 7th Armoured Brigade was unabated. At 2200 hrs., under massive artillery bombardment, the Syrians attacked with T-62s of 3rd Armoured Division in the van. Using their night-fighting equipment, the Syrian tanks closed with the Israelis. Battle was joined at ranges of often less that 100 yards. After three hours the Syrians were forced to withdraw. That night Syrian infantry RPG teams infiltrated the Israeli positions and hit numerous tanks. Few Centurions were destroyed, but 7th Armoured Brigade could not bear any further losses from whatever cause. After the battle subsided the tank crews struggled to repair, refuel and re-arm their vehicles; RPG penetrations were plugged with wooden bungs.

At daybreak the Syrians attacked again. Throughout Monday the brigade repelled assaults by 7th Infantry Division, 3rd Armoured Division and the independent Assad Republican Guard equipped with T-62s. By nightfall Ben Gal and his men were close to exhaustion. They had been awake for 51 hours and fighting for 44 with no time even to eat. The brigade had lost some 50 dead and a large number of wounded, nearly all from artillery fire. That night, taking advantage of their superior night-fighting equipment, the Syrians launched yet another attack towards 'Booster'. The Israeli defence held firm.

As the dawn mists lifted on Tuesday morning an artillery bombardment, the most accurate and intense so far, fell upon 7th Armoured Brigade. As the salvoes of Katyusha rockets and shells rained down, a force of 100 tanks and numerous APCs advanced once more into the 'Valley of Tears'. The Centurions opened fire at maximum range, but as quickly as the Syrian tanks were knocked out, others appeared in their place. To the north, the Assad Republican Guard attempted to bypass Hermonit while waves of Syrian armour closed with the Israeli positions behind the saddle overlooking the valley. The Syrian tanks burst over the rise and became hopelessly intermingled with the Israeli Centurions. Supporting artillery of both sides pounded the battlefield striking friend and foe alike. 7th Armoured Brigade was now fighting through 360 degrees at the limits of mental and physical endurance. As the battle neared its fearful climax, Ben Gal doubted whether the attack could be contained and sought permission to withdraw. Only seven Centurions remained operational, with on average three or four shells left in each tank. At this moment the remnants of the 'Barak' Brigade, with 11 battle-scarred Centurions, struck the Syrian flank near 'Booster', destroying 30 tanks in the initial clash. Even now 7th Armoured Brigade trembled on the verge of collapse. Ben Gal informed Eytan that it was no longer possible to hold out. At this critical juncture a radio message from one of the surrounded infantry strongpoints reported that the Syrian columns were withdrawing. The battle was over.

The Centurions cautiously followed the fleeing Syrians through the devastated 'Valley of Tears', where 260 main battle tanks and as many other AFVs lay abandoned or destroyed, victims of the superlative training and skill of the Israeli 7th Armoured Brigade. On the edge of the anti-tank ditch the exhausted tank crews halted while Israeli artillery bombarded the withdrawing columns. Over the radio Brig. Eytan told Ben Gal and his men: 'You have saved the people of Israel.'

There followed days of bitter and hard-fought battles as the Israelis launched their offensive into Syria, but none could compare with the defensive battle of 7th Armoured Brigade. It had fought for four days and three nights without respite against overwhelming odds in an area some 12 miles wide by up to two miles deep. A major factor in the epic defence was the performance of the Centurion. The Israelis had been well satisfied with Centurion since the Six-Day War but while its mobility and firepower were comparable to other tanks employed by the Armoured Corps, it was the Centurion's ability to withstand battle damage that proved decisive and won the unstinting praise of their crews. The Soviet 115mm U5-T smoothbore gun had proved less effective

An Israeli tank commander, mortally wounded in the throat by shrapnel from a Sagger missile, is lifted from the turret of his Upgraded Centurion during the battle around Hushniyam, 10 October 1973. The high death toll among tank commanders was a heavy price for Israel to bear as they represent some of their ablest most technically proficient personnel, vital both to the Army and to Israeli industry. The radio aerial base is wrapped in polythene to protect it from the elements. (Photographers International)

than expected in the Golan fighting. The buffeting cross-winds of the plateau severely reduced the accuracy of the fin-stabilised projectiles at ranges over 1,500 metres. However, when they did strike a target their penetrative power was awesome. A Centurion crew recall being struck by an APFSDS round which pierced the mantlet, passed between the loader and commander and out through the rear of the turret, leaving only its characteristic star-shaped penetration holes. Against the Soviet-supplied tanks the L7 105mm gun of Centurion (and Patton) proved entirely satisfactory. Israeli tank crews found that the stowage of ammunition and fuel behind the glacis plate alongside the driver's position was especially vulnerable to HEAT rounds causing a devastating internal explosion. Even against the thick armour of the

T-62, a glancing hit from an APDS round was often sufficient to detonate the stowed rounds in the turret rear.

This aspect of ammunition stowage was a crucial factor in many of the tank casualties of the October War. Much research and development effort has been expended in subsequent tank designs to improve the 'survivability' of tanks in battle by incorporating safer stowage of ammunition and fuel in separated compartments, together with sophisticated fire suppression systems. The Centurion design ensured that no main armament rounds were stowed above the level of the turret ring and that fuel was separated from the ammunition behind a fireproof bulkhead, so only a fraction of penetrations resulted in ammunition fires. Israeli statistics reveal that on average every Centurion employed on the Golan was hit three times by rounds of varying calibres, yet only 60 Centurions (less than 10 per cent of those available to the Israelis) were damaged beyond repair in the whole course of the war in Sinai and the Golan. The controversy surrounding the inflammable hydraulic fluid used in the turret traverse system

A column of Meteor-engined Centurions and reconnaissance jeeps pass the blazing remains of a BTR-50 PU command vehicle and abandoned T-62As during the Israeli offensive into Syria. The petrol-engined Centurion may be identified from the rear by the hull configuration and by the two water jerrycans on the turret rear. The Upgraded Centurion has a stowage basket on the rear of the turret. (Israeli Army)

Centurions were also employed in Sinai and were among the first tanks to cross the Suez Canal at Deversoir during Gen. 'Arik' Sharon's offensive 'into Africa'. Both these tanks were built prior to 1951 yet over 20 years on, in a much modified form, the Centurion emerged as the outstanding tank of the October War, testimony to a remarkable AFV. (Israeli Army)

The price of war. Rent asunder by internal explosion, an Upgraded Centurion lies abandoned near Nafekh, destroyed in the savage fighting of Sunday, 7 October 1973. (Photographers International)

of the M48 and M60 is well known. Coupled with the stowage of main armament ammunition in the turret, the 'survivability' record of the M48 and M60 left much to be desired. A grim riddle that circulated among the Israeli Armoured Corps after the war illustrates the problem graphically. Said to have originated among Centurion crews, it went: 'What is the difference between a Patton and a Ronson lighter?', to which the answer ran – 'Nothing, except a Patton always lights first time.'

On account of these factors Centurion emerged as the best tank of the war and remains a firm favourite within the Israeli Armoured Corps. A further instance of the high regard in which

Centurion is held manifested itself subsequently. On induction into the Israeli Defence Forces an Israeli citizen may choose which branch of the services he wishes to join. Provided he has the necessary aptitude and qualifications he may opt for one of the élite fighting arms such as fighter pilot, paratrooper or tank crewman. However, Israeli law stipulates that an only son of a family cannot serve in such formations without the written permission of both parents. Following the October War, it was not uncommon for parents to withold permission for their son wishing to become a tank crewman unless he joined a Centurion unit.

The Plates

Front cover: *Centurion Mark 5 of 4 Troop, 'A' Squadron, 6th Royal Tank Regiment, commanded by Cpl. Sturgess during Operation 'Musketeer'; Treaty Road, Suez Canal, 6 November 1956*

The Centurions of 6th Royal Tank Regiment during the Suez landings were Mark 5s reworked from Mark 3 standard, with the substitution of the co-axial 7.92mm Besa machine gun by the .30cal. Browning. 'Iron Mouse' is finished in overall sand yellow and illustrates the markings peculiar to Operation 'Musketeer'. On the forward slope of the turret roof is painted a large white 'H' – an air recognition sign; emblazoned on all French and British vehicles, the 'H' stands for 'Hamilcar', the original name given to Operation 'Musketeer'. The black stripe around the turret is a mutual recognition device carried by French and British tanks, a necessary precaution as the Egyptians were known to have some Centurions in service. On the turret side bins the squadron triangle symbol enclosing the vehicle callsign '4B' follows the standard pattern, with '4 Bravo' signifying the third tank in 4 Troop. In 6 RTR troops are numbered sequentially, e.g. 11 Troop is 3 Troop, 'C' Sqn. The markings of 'A' Sqn. are red, as is the aerial pennant. Squadron colours follow the code of armoured regiment seniority. The long weeks of waiting in Malta prior to the landings are reflected in the numerous names applied to the tank. On the left front trackguard (as viewed) is 'Babbs?' – suggesting a degree of doubt on the part of the crewman as to the constancy of the young lady's affections. 'PAT' (right trackguard) and 'BIG BERTHA' (midway along the gun barrel) are painted in more confident style. To the left of the vehicle registration number 00ZR95 is the unit insignia, and to the right the formation sign of 3rd Infantry Division – the 'Iron Division'.

A1: Centurion Mark 1 of 'B' Squadron, 1st Royal Tank Regiment; Detmold, Germany, 1947

The Centurion entered service with the British Army in December 1946. One of the first units to receive the tank was 1st Royal Tank Regiment, known at the time as the 'Prime Panzers'. The vehicle is painted Deep Bronze Green and carries the famous red jerboa of 7th Armoured Division. On the left of the glacis plate is the Royal Armoured Corps arm-of-service flash surmounted by a white bar with the legend '1 R Tks' (the correct abbreviation of 1st Royal Tank Regiment) superimposed in black. The name 'Mechile' on the turret sides indicates a Centurion of 'B' Sqn., as their tanks were named after regimental battles of the North African campaign and Italy. 'A' Sqn. tanks displayed those of 'A' Bn. during the Great War, while 'C' Sqn. named theirs after battles in North-West Europe. Shipping instructions are painted on the right front trackguard indicating the port of destination – Hamburg; the manifest number FSO 9925/3; and, on the side of the trackguard stowage bins, the directive 'NOT TO BE STOWED ON DECK'. Other markings include the vehicle registration number T351822 on the top right of the glacis plate below which is stencilled 'THIS VEHICLE IS FILLED WITH ANTI-FREEZE 1/8/46 & MUST NOT BE DRAINED'.

A2: Centurion Mark 3 of 'C' Squadron, 8th King's Royal Irish Hussars, commanded by Capt. George Strachan MC; Yongdungpo, Korea, 11 February 1951

The first Centurion to fire a shot in anger was 'Caughoo', an early production Centurion Mark 3 belonging to 'C' Sqn. HQ Troop, 8 KRIH and commanded by Capt. George Strachan MC. As befitted a famous cavalry regiment, the names of 8th Hussars tanks in Korea were equestrian in nature. 'A' (traditionally known in the KRIH as 'R') and 'C' Sqns. named their tanks after racehorses beginning with the squadron letter, while 'B' Sqn. named theirs after hunts, hunters and hounds; e.g. 'Alycidon', 'Aly Sloper', 'April Fool', 'Berkeley', 'Bosun', 'Boxer', 'Colorado', 'Cameronian' and 'Colonist'. The names of Regimental HQ vehicles began with the letter H, e.g. 'Humorist', 'Halcyon' and 'Hurry On' – the traditional name of the regimental commander's tank. During the initial mobile phase of the Korean War, all Allied vehicles displayed prominent white stars – the recognition sign of the United Nations Forces. In 1948 the wartime 'T' number registration system for tanks was superseded by a civilian-type plate bearing numerals and letters. The registration number of 'Caughoo' is 02ZR58, carried on the rear hull plate, and on a black strip on the turret sides and lower front hull. The vehicle callsign, 'SA' within a circle, denotes the second tank of 'C' Sqn. HQ Troop. It is displayed on a black metal plate on the centre bazooka plate and turret rear. The loose metal plates were often lost in action and 'Caughoo' lacked one on the other side. On the left front trackguard (as viewed) is the RAC flash with unit serial '41' superimposed in black, while on the right is the 'frozen orifice' formation sign of 29th Infantry Brigade, a white ring on a black square. The tank is liberally stowed with tarpaulins, bed rolls and crew comforts to ward off the bitter cold of the Korean winter, as well as water jerrycans, rimless RAC helmets and discarded ammunition boxes as extra stowage bins. The generous allocation (or redistribution) of American stores made these essential items. On the cooling air deflector beneath the rear hull plate is the black and white convoy distance marker, common to all Centurions.

B1: Centurion Mark 3 of 3 Troop, 'C' Squadron, 1st Royal Tank Regiment, commanded by Sgt. A. Wallace MM; The Hook, Korea, 28 May 1953
'Arromanches', a mid-production Centurion Mark 3 of 1st Royal Tank Regiment, was commanded by Sergeant Wallace at the battle of the Hook. Finished in standard Deep Bronze Green, the tank is named after the French town of D-Day fame. Over the barrel of the 20pdr. is an American searchlight which was destroyed soon after battle was joined. On the barrel itself the gunner has painted the name of his girlfriend – 'Lily'. Several Centurions in Korea supplemented their firepower with .50cal. M2HB Brownings, obtained from Americans or Canadians in exchange for Scotch or beer. A spare roadwheel is hung on the rear hull to replace any destroyed by gunfire. Note the damage to the front bazooka plate – it was not unknown for Centurions to be stripped of all bazooka plates, trackguards and stowage bins by enemy artillery. The vehicle registration number 02BA37 is displayed below the turret stowage bins on a black strip, and on the rear hull. On the front left trackguard (as viewed) and rear hull plate is the RAC flash with the unit serial '41' superimposed in white. The name of the

driver's girlfriend, 'Pearl', appears on the glacis plate forward of his position. Sgt. Wallace was awarded the Military Medal for his gallantry in the Hook battle.

B2: Centurion ARV Mark 1 of 'C' Squadron, 1st Royal Tank Regiment, commanded by Sgt. T. George, RNZAC; Gloster Valley, Korea, 1953
The pressing need in Korea for a more powerful armoured recovery vehicle than the Churchill ARV Mark 2 prompted the production of a stop-gap design pending the introduction of a purpose-built vehicle. Based on the hulls of redundant Centurions Mark 1 and 2, the ARV Mark 1 proved to be an effective machine. The ARV is painted overall Deep Bronze Green and carries on the side stowage bin the 'C' Sqn. sign in red, outlined in white for greater clarity. Commanded by Sgt. George, on attachment from the Royal New Zealand Armoured Corps, the crew have advertised their trade with the slogan 'You Call – We Haul' on the gun planks stowed on the front superstructure. Markings include the insignia of 1st British Commonwealth Division on the right front trackguard, with the Royal Electrical and Mechanical Engineers (REME) flash and unit serial on the left.

One criticism made of the vehicle in Korea concerned the lack of observation devices when 'closed down' under fire. This was overcome by installing a gun-tank cupola over the commander's position. Several ARVs in Korea were fitted with dummy guns to make them less conspicuous in the front line. The modification, which consisted of a piece of tubing, was known as the 'Salmon Gun' since the tins of fish purporting to be salmon which came in the ration packs were universally loathed and, being of similar diameter to the tubing, were disposed of in the obvious manner. On one occasion a Centurion ARV descending a steep hill braked sharply, cascading tins of 'salmon' at the feet of a baffled yet delighted group of Korean children.

C1: Centurion Mark 5 of 10 Troop, 'C' Squadron, 4th Royal Tank Regiment, commanded by Sgt. 'Jake' Jacobs; West Berlin, 22 August 1961
This Centurion Mark 5 with 20pdr. A Type barrel is shown on the Bismarckstrasse in West

Berlin during an alert following the sealing of the Soviet sector behind the Berlin Wall. 'C' Sqn. of 4th Royal Tank Regiment provided armoured support to the Berlin Independent Infantry Brigade Group. The colour scheme of overall US Olive Drab is peculiar to British military vehicles in Berlin during this period. On the left trackguard is the bridging classification sign. Below the registration number on the lower front hull is the Union Flag common to all British vehicles in BAOR, distinguishing them from other NATO nations. The unit insignia and formation insignia of the Berlin Brigade appear either side of the registration plate 05BA46. The vehicle name 'Diehard' is painted on the sides of the trackguard stowage bins; tank names in 4 RTR have traditionally begun with the fourth letter of the alphabet. Another tradition is the 'Chinese eye' painted on the forward face of the turret stowage bins. It first appeared during the First World War on a

Tank Mark IV of 'F' Battalion which was paid for by a Chinese businessman. Later it was carried by tanks of 4th Bn., Royal Tank Corps and subsequently by all tanks of 4 RTR. Other markings include the 'C' Sqn. tactical sign in white, and the vehicle callsign, a plain white '2', on the black-painted jerrycan at turret rear. All of them were kept in immaculate condition, with such details as black-painted mantlet cover and alternate red/white striped radio aerials.

One interesting variant of Centurion in Korea was the Centurion Tug, a conversion of battle-damaged gun tanks to carry supplies to hilltop positions inaccessible to wheeled vehicles. South Korean porters load a Centurion Tug of 8 KRIH under supervision from men of 3rd Battalion Royal Australian Regiment (3 RAR). The Australians frequently employed Tugs to carry defence stores up the hills; it was some time before the 8th Hussars discovered that beneath a thin layer of ammunition or trip flares there was crate upon crate of 'Asahi' beer. The Australians insisted that these were an integral part of their defensive plan! (Australian War Memorial)

C2: Centurion Mark 10 of 4 Troop, 'C' Squadron, 16th/5th Lancers, commanded by Cpl. Finney during Operation 'Armadillo's Delight'; Wadi Misrah, Radfan, 19 May 1964

The tank is finished in the standard camouflage scheme of sand-yellow and black stripes common to British military vehicles based in Aden. At any one time one squadron of the resident armoured regiment served with the Royal Navy Amphibious Warfare Squadron, whose rôle was to patrol the Persian Gulf to meet any emergency arising in the area. One of the perennial trouble spots was the Iraq/Kuwait border, and as the Iraqis were equipped with Centurion tanks a broad white band was painted on the rear bazooka plates of British Centurions as a recognition device.

Centurions Mk.10 of 4 Troop 'C' Sqn. 16th/5th Lancers firing on rebel positions in the Wadi Misrah, 19 May 1964, the last occasion that British tanks have fired in anger. (Soldier)

Obviously old 'Cent' hands, the crew have painted the tank's registration number 02DA96 at the top of each bazooka plate so that they are not lost among the many others that litter a tank park during maintenance sessions. On the rear hull plate, partly obscured by the spare roadwheel, is the unit insignia of a white '2' on the RAC flash, and the 'black dhow' formation sign of the Aden Garrison. The black and white convoy distance marker is just visible beneath the towing pintle. These markings are repeated on the lower front hull together with the bridging classification sign – see detail view. Beside the obvious need for extra water jerrycans when operating 'up country', the spare roadwheels were essential items in the Radfan where the appalling terrain shredded rubber tyres and distorted tracks to an alarming degree. Note the split hatches of the commander's cupola, characteristic of Centurions Mark 8, 10 and 13.

D1: Centurion Mark 7 of Maj.Gen. Rajinder Singh, GOC Indian 1st Armoured Division; North Punjab, September 1965

The tank of Maj. Gen. 'Sparrow' Rajinder Singh, General Officer Commanding 1st Armoured Division in the Sialkot battles during the Indo-Pakistani War of September 1965. The vehicle registration number KX261 appears on the lower front hull and trackguard stowage bins. The trumpeting elephant insignia of 1st Armoured Division is borne on the front right trackguard. On the opposite trackguard is the black square of Divisional HQ with the serial '25' in white. These insignia are repeated on the rear hull plate just above the level of the towing pintle. The elephant appears immediately to its left, '25' immediately to its right; immediately right of this is '(arrow) KX/261' in two lines on a black background. Between the headlights and on each turret side is the vehicle name 'Ankush'. This is the Persian/Urdu word for an elephant goad carried by a *mahout* to guide and encourage his charge, an appropriate name for a command tank. It was customary for only command tanks to display such names: regimental commanders named their

Kuwaiti Centurion Mk.8/1 crewed by men of 3rd Carabiniers during the Iraqi confrontation of 1961. Following the independence declaration of Kuwait, the neighbouring state of Iraq laid claim to the oil-rich kingdom. British troops were hastily despatched to Kuwait in July, including the Centurions of 'C' Sqn. 3rd Carabiniers. Other members of the regiment manned Centurions that were held in storage in Kuwait for just such an eventuality. After several weeks in the appalling desert heat in temperatures as high as 140°F, tension subsided. Interestingly, the Iraqis were also equipped with Centurions at this time. (Soldier)

tanks after battle honours. The overall drab green colour scheme is enlivened by the pale yellow solid circle air recognition sign on the turret roof. After the 1965 war the Indian Armoured Corps adopted four official disruptive camouflage schemes of either sand yellow, khaki or light green over the vehicle base colour, depending on the location and season. Squadron insignia and callsigns follow the British pattern.

D2: Centurion Mark 5 of Israeli Defence Forces, Six-Day War; Sinai, June 1967

This modified Centurion Mark 5 bears the chevron and stripe markings typical of Israeli tanks during the Six-Day War. The significance of these markings has not been revealed by the IDF and it is not the author's intention to divulge classified military information; suffice it to say, no published reference to date has provided a full interpretation.

The Centurion was initially viewed with disfavour by Israeli tank crews as being too complex, but once they had mastered the intricacies of the vehicle it became and remains a popular tank. During the Six-Day War it was the only tank, save for one company of M48 Pattons, to mount the highly effective L7 105mm gun, a superior weapon to any other tank gun in the conflict. From February 1963 Israeli Centurions were up-gunned with the 105mm and by the Six-Day War most of them had undergone conversion. No Israeli Centurions were fitted with the French L/51 105mm gun, a weapon of inferior capability to the L7. The separate view shows the unit insignia of the famed Israeli 7th Armoured Brigade, reserved for ceremonial purposes. Apart from the upwards-pointing chevron on the bazooka plates and the gun stripes, the only marking is the white-on-black registration '811909 *tsadi*'.

E1: Centurion ARV Mark 2 attached to 'C' Squadron, 1st Armoured Regiment, RAAC, commanded by Sgt. P. De Jong, RAEME; Fire Support Base 'Coral', Bien Hoa Province, South Vietnam, May 1968

Of all the specialized vehicles based on Centurion, none was more important than the armoured recovery vehicle intended to retrieve disabled tanks under hostile fire. In Vietnam few tank operations were conducted without the support of an ARV and an M113A1 Fitter's Track. Manned by personnel of the Royal Australian Electrical and Mechanical Engineers (RAEME), the Centurion ARV Mark 2 was constantly in action both in the assault and the recovery of casualties bogged in the mire of the Vietnamese countryside. Each squadron in Vietnam enjoyed the support of two ARVs. Soon after arrival in Vietnam, armoured extensions were welded to the rear stowage bins to provide protection from small arms fire for counter-mine engineers and tracker-dog teams who rode on the rear decks. A gunshield was also fitted to the commander's cupola-mounted machine gun. The base colour, Australian olive drab, is masked beneath the red dust characteristic of much of Vietnam. Markings are

limited to the vehicle registration number 169122 front and rear, the vehicle name 'Costa Bower', and the callsign '38B'. The initial number denotes 'C' Sqn., '8' the recovery section and 'Bravo' the ARV: '38A' was the callsign of the M113A1 Fitter's Track. '38B' is applied freehand on each side of the vehicle in subdued black, so denying an aiming point to enemy RPG teams. The vehicle name painted freehand in neat white capital letters on the sides of the trackguard stowage bins, is Gaelic for 'death carriage', a mythical contraption driven by a headless horseman. Over the crew compartment is a nylon shade giving protection from sun and rain.

E2: Centurion Mark 5/1 (Aust) of 1 Troop, 'C' Squadron, 1st Armoured Regiment, RAAC, commanded by Lt. G. McCormack; Long Dien, Phuoc Tuy Province, South Vietnam, September 1968

In 1967 the Centurions destined for Vietnam were modified at 3rd Base Workshops, Bandiana, with the addition of infra-red night fighting equipment, supplementary armour on the glacis plate, a .50cal. Browning ranging gun and a 100-gallon fuel tank on the rear hull plate. Designated Centurion Mark 5/1 (Australian), four troops of these gun tanks were deployed to South Vietnam in 1968. The vehicle callsign '31' is prominently displayed on the rear fuel tank and transmission decks. The latter would be clearly visible to an airborne observer guiding the tanks through difficult terrain. Denoting 1st Troop Leader of 'C' Sqn., the callsign was repeated on a black metal plate attached centrally to the turret rear stowage basket. The registration number 169049 is painted in white on the rear fuel tank and top right of the glacis plate. Below the registration number is the arm-of-service flash of the Royal Australian Armoured Corps with the unit serial '106' superimposed in white. This is repeated on the top left of the glacis plate. Between the turret stowage bins is painted the insignia of 1 Troop, a yellow numeral '1' beneath a red leaping kangaroo surmounted by a black umbrella. The red kangaroo was initially painted on all 1st Australian Task Force vehicles; this caused the South Vietnamese peasants, who had never seen a kangaroo and therefore had no comparable word for the animal in their language, to nickname them 'Red

Rats'. The addition of the umbrella reflected the troop leader's penchant for directing tanks in battle while wielding a black umbrella!

F1: Centurion Mark 7 of 40th Armoured Brigade; Battle of Ramtha, Jordanian Civil War, 22 September 1970

After the Six-Day War the Palestine Liberation Organization (PLO) created guerilla bases in the Kingdom of Jordan from which they launched raids into the West Bank and Israel. By the summer of 1970 the PLO had become a major force in Middle-East politics, openly flouting the authority of the Jordanian government. This culminated in the hijacking of three Western airliners to Dawson's Field, a desert airstrip near Amman, on 6 September 1970. While the drama unfolded in the desert in front of the cameras of the world press, the Jordanian Army, which had been ordered not to interfere, became increasingly restive. During a parade by an armoured regiment, King Hussein was outraged to see brassieres fluttering from the radio aerials of the officers' Centurions. Demanding an explanation the King was informed by a tank commander – 'You have

After the October War the Upgraded Centurion was further modified with additional armour on glacis plate and turret roof, a machine gun at the loader's hatches, AN VSS-3A infrared searchlight, and latterly a thermal sleeve for the 105mm gun. An Upgraded Centurion at the Good Fence returns from operations in Lebanon against PLO guerilla bases, September 1977. (Israeli Army)

made women out of us. You won't let us fight.'

Within days martial law was imposed and the Army was unleashed against the guerilas. The Centurions of 40th Armoured Brigade were moved to the northern border to stop supplies and reinforcements reaching the guerilas from Syria. On 21 September a large Syrian tank formation from 67th and 88th Armoured Brigades, with infantry and artillery, including elements of the Palestine Liberation Army (PLA), crossed the border at Ramtha. At dawn on the 22nd, a tank battle developed between the Jordanian 40th and 60th Armoured Brigades and the Syrian/PLA invasion force. On the following day the Jordanians announced that the Syrians had been expelled from the country, and claimed 100 enemy tanks destroyed for a loss of 19 of their own. The Centurion is painted overall in a slightly 'pink' sand shade, with large irregular green stripes. Markings include the formation sign of 40th Armoured Brigade and the registration plate of the vehicle number below the Arabic word *Al-Jaish* 'Army'. These are repeated on the left and right front trackguards, respectively. Jordanian tanks carry the vehicle callsign, unknown in this instance, on a black metal plate on the turret rear. Typical would be an Arabic '21' in white, the plate being about half the depth of the turret. The patch views show the Brigade sign as in 1967; as in 1970; and as currently seen.

F2: Centurion AVRE of 26th Armoured Engineer Squadron; Operation 'Motorman', Creggan Estate, Londonderry, 31 July 1972

The largest operation conducted by the British Army since Suez was Operation 'Motorman'. The object of the operation was to restore control in those areas of Ulster that were dominated by extremists, especially the Creggan and Bogside areas of Londonderry, and the Andersonstown and Ballymurphy areas of Belfast. At 0400 hrs. on 31 July 1972 four Centurion AVREs, their turrets traversed and guns shrouded beneath tarpaulins, entered the so-called 'No-Go' area around the Rossville Flats and Creggan estate in Londonderry. Within hours all objectives had been seized by the security forces. Meanwhile the Centurion AVREs expeditiously demolished the reinforced barricades that otherwise would have taken days to dismantle. The Centurion AVRE was employed for this task because it was believed that the barricades were mined and only an AVRE had sufficient armour protection against this threat. The AVRE is finished in the standard British Army disruptive camouflage of matt black stripes over a base colour of flat green. The vehicle registration number 09BA64 appears on the rear hull, and in one line at top right of the glacis plate. There is little doubt as to the identity of the users of the Centurion AVRE, as the bazooka plates testify. Below the title is a decal of the ship's crest of HMS *Fearless*. The Landing Platform Dock (LPD) HMS *Fearless* transported the AVREs to and from Ulster for Operation 'Motorman' and the ship's crest was affixed to each side of them before landing. Although the vehicles were normally crewed by six sappers, only three crewmen (commander, driver and wireless operator)

manned them during 'Motorman' for fear of casualties from boobytrapped barricades. After they had successfully completed their tasks, the Centurion AVREs were re-embarked on LCTs by 1215 hrs. and returned to HMS *Fearless*.

G1: Upgraded Centurion attached to Israeli 79th Armoured Brigade; attack towards Kuneitra, Golan Heights, Wednesday, 10 October 1973

By October 1973 almost half of Israel's Centurions had been modified with the Teledyne Continental AVDS-1790-2A diesel engine, Allison CD-850-6A automatic transmission and other modifications enhancing their speed, range and performance. The Israeli Ordnance Corps designation of the vehicle is 'Upgraded Centurion'. This tank was attached to the 79th Armoured Brigade, a reserve formation in the division of Maj.Gen. Dan Laner, the oustanding exponent of armoured warfare in the October War. The system of markings is an extension of previous practice, and includes the vehicle callsign '*Aleph* 2' on a loose khaki cloth tied to the turret stowage basket. A fluorescent yellow/pink air recognition panel is tied to the turret roof. The Upgraded Centurion is identified by the enlarged rear hull, air filter boxes on the trackguards, revised headlight assemblies and turret stowage basket.

G2: Upgraded Centurion, Israeli Armoured Corps; Operation 'Litani River' against PLO bases, Southern Lebanon, March 1978

The Israeli Armoured Corps remains the major user of Centurion, and approximately 1,000 are in service. Since the Yom Kippur War of October 1973 further modifications have been made to the Upgraded Centurions, including additional armour protection on the glacis plate and the turret roof. The frightening casualty rate among commanders led to the appearance of a new cupola hatch known as the 'Tal cupola', which permits direct vision while retaining overhead cover. A machine gun has been mounted at the loader's hatches, to counter infantry anti-tank teams. Contrary to many published references, the Israeli Centurion is not known as the 'Ben-Gurion'; among Zahal armoured personnel it is called '*Shot*', which is Hebrew for 'whip'.

This Centurion illustrates the latest Israeli tank

markings; their neatness and regularity of application suggests a regular rather than a reserve unit. Their interpretation is a matter for speculation. One logical explanation might be that the outline of the formation sign on the right track guard, a star in this case, identifies a brigade, with the enclosed numeral identifying a battalion within the brigade. The two bars on the left trackguard might identify the company, as the stripes round the gun barrels may formerly have done; they are followed by the platoon letter and tank number. The devices which appear on the front faces of the turret bins on each side are unexplained.

The patch view shows the bronze cap badge of the Israeli Armoured Corps, normally worn through a scarlet cloth backing on a black beret.

In the October War there were few recovery vehicles in Israeli armoured formations and tank casualties such as this scarred and battered Centurion had to be towed from the battle area by other gun tanks, thus putting two tanks out of battle while recovery was effected. Both are Meteor-engined versions distinguishable from the front by the unprotected headlights on the glacis plate which replaced the British hooded battle lights. The commander's .50cal. Browning is also indicative of this earlier type. (Israeli Army)

H1: Lieutenant, 1st Royal Tank Regiment; Korea, 1953

British tank crews arrived in Korea with clothing inadequate to meet the rigours of the bitter Siberian cold. In the winter of 1950/51 crewmen wore every stitch of clothing they possessed, including pyjamas, under the one-piece 'pixie' tank suit. More suitable clothing, notably the 'parka', was obtained from US and Canadian sources pending the introduction of purpose-designed British winter uniforms. This troop leader wears a khaki-green two piece combat fatigue outfit which

37

was standard issue during the summer months. Comfort was the primary consideration and dress regulations were generally lax in Korea. His '37 pattern webbing includes compass and ammunition pouches with a .38 Webley revolver in a canvas holster. Headgear is the RTR black beret and 'Fear Naught' cap badge. Over the left shoulder he carries the red lanyard exclusive to 1 RTR and on the upper left arm a cloth brassard displaying the insignia of 1st British Commonwealth Division (see Plate B2). Although 'Cobbly Wobbly' CWW (Cold Wet Winter) boots were issued from 1952, this officer has the standard '36

pattern, above which he sports American web leggings. Following the First World War tradition he carries an ashplant stick to test the 'going' for his tanks. The 'hutchie' or 'basha' in the background, built into the side of a hill, was typical of the living quarters of tank crewmen during the static phase of the Korean War.

H2: Sergeant, RAEME, 1st Armoured Regiment; South Vietnam, 1968

The illustration shows the commander of Australian Centurion ARV Mark 2, 'Costa Bower' (see Plate E1). The light green tropical bush shirt has bleached and faded through repeated washing and the harsh sunlight. Over the left breast pocket the commander's name 'De Jong' has been applied in black ink in US Army style, and over the right pocket is a local laundry mark. Trousers are worn

The war over, training continues in the desert, June 1975. These Israeli Armoured Corps reservists have modified their Upgraded Centurion for a game of basketball between exercises. The Upgraded Centurion may be identified from the front by the fire extinguisher pull handles and American headlight assemblies on the glacis plate. (Israeli Army)

without gaiters, tucked into calf-length black boots. Clear plastic dust goggles are perched on a soft bush hat, and he keeps radio watch with headphones over one ear only so as to be aware of his surroundings. On his right shoulder he wears a cloth brassard showing his rank of sergeant and arm-of-service – Royal Australian Electrical/and Mechanical Engineers. As a personal sidearm in Vietnam Australian tank crewmen were issued with the 9mm Browning Hi-Power automatic in a black leather shoulder holster. Although an effective weapon, it was rarely worn after the first weeks because its chafing encouraged tropical skin rashes, and it was liable to snag when 'bailing-out' in an emergency – this was especially dangerous in the ARV with its narrow No.1 Mk.2 cupola. This particular vehicle commander discontinued wearing a pistol after only a month, preferring the greater firepower of the cupola-mounted .30cal. M1919A4 Browning machine gun. A gunshield, cut from a discarded bazooka plate, has been added to give protection from small arms fire.

H3: 1st Lieutenant and Private, Israeli Armoured Corps; October War, 1973

This Upgraded Centurion crew wear the olive green tank suit which was adopted shortly before the October War. Made of fire-retardant Nomex material, it is akin to the American helicopter crew flying suit developed during the Vietnam War. Both crewmen have American CVC (Combat Vehicle Crewman) helmets with integral headphones and wire boom radio microphone. The helmet is of glass fibre with a black rubber edging, offering 'bump' but not ballistic protection to the wearer. The tank commander is a *Segen* or 1st Lieutenant, signified by the two rank bars on the cloth shoulder strap slip-overs. Normally made in green material, in this instance the rank bars are metal, a popular variation among regular officers of the Israeli Armoured Corps. Webbing is confined to a belt without sidearms; the crew weapon is the 9mm Uzi submachine gun. Crewmen wear black calf-length lace-up rubber-soled boots. In the opening days of the October War the casualty rate among tank commanders rose to alarming proportions. So many of the dead were either decapitated or disfigured beyond

The Centurion will remain in service with the Israeli Armoured Corps for many years to come. These Centurions, during an exercise on the Golan in 1979, are of the latest type with additional armour on the glacis plate, hence the spare tracklinks on the rear hull. Of interest are the loader's machine gun and the new 'Tal cupola'. As an exception to the rule, the nearer Upgraded Centurion has no turret stowage basket. (Israeli Army)

recognition by shrapnel that tank commanders were ordered to wear their 'dog-tag' identity discs around their ankle. The crewmen show the strain and exhaustion from almost continuous fighting on the Golan, but with the usual Israeli bravura in front of a camera the tank commander holds three fingers aloft indicating the number of enemy tanks destroyed in a recent battle.

Notes sur les planches en couleur

Couverture: La bande noir autour de la tourelle et le 'H' blanc sur le toit sont tous les deux des marques de reconnaissance portées par tous les chars français et anglais à Suez. On peut voir l'insigne de la 3ème Division à droite, sur la plaque blindée à l'avant de la coque. Le char a été baptisé 'Iron Mouse' (La Souris de Fer); les autres noms sont ceux des épouses et petites amies des membres de l'équipage.

A1 On peut voir ici l'insigne des 'rats du desert' de la 7th Armoured Division; le char s'appelle 'Mechile'. L'éscadron 'B' de ce régiment nomme ses chars d'après les batailles d'Afrique et d'Italie de la 2e GM. On peut également distinguer l'insigne du Royal Armoured Corps, carré rouge et jaune, la bande blanche du haut portant l'inscription '1 R Tks'. **A2** 'Caughoo', baptisé d'après un cheval de course, porte l'insigne en forme d'étoile de même que tous les véhicles des Nations Unies en Corée. L'indicatif d'appel du char est 'SA', qui est celui du deuxième char d'Etat Major d'éscadron 'C'. '41' sur l'insigne RAC rouge et jaune identifie le régiment; et enfin le cercle blanc sur fond noir, la British 29th Infantry Brigade, à laquelle le regiment était attaché.

B1 Projecteur américain fixé au dessus du canon. Le projecteur fut détruit pendant la bataille de ce jour. Le nom du char est 'Arromanches'. 'Lily' sur le canon et 'Pearl' devant la trappe du conducteur indiquent les objets de poursuites de l'équipage! L.avant gauche et l'arrière de la coque porte le numéro '41' sur carres rouge et jaune, non visible ici. **B2** L'insigne 'C' Sqn. circulaire en rouge sur les coffres d'arrimage latérale est visible ici; sur les gardes-boue avant droite et gauche on peut voir l'insigne des Royal Electrical and Mechanical Engineers, qui équipaient ce véhicule de récupération; également, 1st British Commonwealth Division. La devise en est: 'Vous Appelez, Nous Remorquons'.

C1 Le numéro de code du régiment sur l'insigne rouge et jaune RAC et l'insigne de la Berlin Brigade apparaissent de chaque côté du numéro de registration; en dessous le pavillon britannique, qui nous perment d'identifier les véhicules de BAOR. L'emblème en 'œil chinois' sur les coffres de tourelles était porté depuis la 1e GM par les chars de cette unité. Le numero '2' est le numéro d'appel du char, peint à l'intérieur du cercle de 'C' Sqn. **C2** Couleurs de camouflage réglementaires des chars britanniques à Aden, avec les bandes blanches sur les côtés pour empêcher de les confondre avec les Centurions de l'armée iraquenne. L'emblème représentant un *dhow* noir est celui de la garnison d'Aden.

D1 Le numero KX261 apparait sur le devant, les côtés et l'arrière de la coque. 'Ankush', qui signifie un aiguillon à éléphant, est le nom du char, approprié au commandant d'une division dont l'emblème est un éléphant; seuls les chars de commande avaient un nom. Remarquez les signes jaunes de reconnaissance aérienne sur le toit de la tourelle. **D2** La signification des inscriptions israéliennes de chevrons et de rayures sur l'affût des canons n'a jamais été confirmée; des combinations variées permettaient d'identifier les bataillons et les compagnies. Le détail nous montre l'insigne de la 7th Armoured Brigade, qui n'était porté que lors des cérémonies.

E1 Le char s'appelle 'Costa Bower', nom gaélique d'un chariot mortuaire légendaire. L'insigne '38B' identifie le 'C' Sqn. (3); la section de recuperation (8); et le ARV (B). La peinture vert olive est presqu'entièrement recouverte par la poussière rouge du Viet-Nam. **E2** On identifie le chef du peloton par le numéro '31' – 1 Troop, 'C' Sqn. L'emblème de kangourou est celui de la 1st Australian Task Force, avec le numéro de troop rajouté. Peinture verte couverte de poussière rouge.

F1 Ce char, en camouflage normale jordanien vert et jaune sable, s'est battu contre les forces syriennes. L'emblème rouge et jaune est l'insigne de la 40th Brigade; les insignes plus petits en sont des versions plus anciennes; celui de gauche était utilisé pendant la guerre de 1967. **F2** Ce char est un de quatre qui ont servis à renverser les barricades en Ulster; avec son equipage de Royal Engineers, il porte également l'insigne du bateau HMS Fearless qui transporta les chars en Ulster – les marins les ont collés sur le char.

G1 Le numéro d'appel individuel 'Aleph 2' est inscrit sur une bande de tissu; la signification des autres inscriptions n'a jamais été éclaircie. **G2** La signification des inscriptions n'a pas été éclaircie. La vue de détail montre l'insigne de casquette du corps blindé 'Zahal'.

H1 Uniforme mixte anglais-américains; cordon rouge du regiment, et insigne de la division sur brassard. **H2** Le commandant du char sur la plaque E1 porte sur son brassard les chevrons indiquant son rang et le nom du regiment. **H3** Combinaison à l'épreuve du feu, et casques avec équipement intégral de radio, tous deux de fabrication américain, acquis par Israel juste avant la guerre de 1973. Les deux galons sur la patte d'épaule de l'officer sont celles d'un *Segen* – lieutenant. Notez les plaques d'identité portées autour de la cheville, plutôt qu'au cou, à cause des nombreuses pertes furd sux blessures à la tête pendant cette guerre.

Farbtafeln

Vorderer Umschlag: Sowohl das schwarze Band um den Turm, als auch das weisse 'H' auf dem Dach sind Erkennungszeichen, die von allen französischen und englischen Panzern bei Suez getragen wurden. Am rechten Ende der vorderen Platte des Rumpfes ist das Abzeichen der 3rd Division. Die Mannschaft nannte ihren Panzer 'Iron Mouse' (eiserne Maus); die anderen Namen sind die der Ehefrauen und Freundinnen der Mannschaft.

A1 Sichtbar sind die Wüstenratten-Abzeichen der 7th Armoured Division; der Panzername 'Mechile' – der 'B' Kompanie dieses Regiments nannte die Panzer nach den Schlachten im 2. Weltkrieg in Afrika und Italien, und das Abzeichen des Royal Armoured Corps auf einem rot/gelben Quadrat, der weisse obere Streifen trägt '1 R Tks'. **A2** 'Caughoo', benannt nach einem Rennpferd, trägt das Sternenzeichen aller UN-Fahrzeuge in Korea. 'SA' ist das Panzerfunkrufzeichen, welches den zweiten Panzer, HQ Zug, 'C' Kompanie erkennen lässt. Die Nummer '41' auf dem rot/gelben RAC Zeichen, lässt das Regiment erkennen; und der weisse Kreis auf schwarzem Grund, die British 29th Infantry Brigade, dem das Regiment angeschlossen war.

B1 Amerikanischer Scheinwerfer über dem Geschütz hinzugefügt – der Scheinwerfer wurde in den Kämpfen an diesem Tag zerstört. Der Panzername ist 'Arromanches'; 'Lily' auf dem Geschütz und 'Pearl' auf der glacis vor der Luke des Fahrers, lassen die Objekte der Zuneigung der Mannschaft erkennen! Unsichtbar ist hier die Nr. '41' auf rot/gelben Quadraten links vorne und hinten auf dem Rumpf. **B2** 'C' Sqn. kreisförmiges Zeichen in rot auf den Seiten der Staubehälter; auf den linken und rechten vorderen Kettenschutzen, das Abzeichen der Royal Electrical and Mechanical Ingenieure, die dieses Bergungsfahrzeug bemannten; und 1st British Commonwealth Division. Das Motto heisst 'Sie rufen, wir schleppen'.

C1 Die Code-Nummer des Regiments auf dem rot/gelben RAC Abzeichen und das Wappen der Berlin Brigade, erscheinen auf beiden Seiten des Kennzeichenschildes; darunter ist der Union Jack, die Fahrzeuge der BAOR identifizierend. Das 'chinesische Augen' Abzeichen an den Turmbehältern wurde seit dem 1. Weltkrieg von Panzern dieser Einheit getragen. '2' ist das individuelle Panzerfunkrufzeichen, innen in dem Kreis des 'C' Sqn. gemalt. **C2** Die normale Tarnfarbe für britische Panzer in Aden mit Weissen Seitenstreifen um eine Verwechslung mit den Centurions der irakischen Armee zu vermeiden. Das schwarze dhow Zeichen ist das der Garnison in Aden.

D1 Die Nummer KX261 erscheint vorne, auf der Seite und hinten am Rumpf. 'Ankush' – d.h. ein Stachelstock fur Elefanten – ist der Panzername, geeignet für den Kommandeur einer Division, deren Wappen ein Elefant war; nur Kommando-Panzer hatten Namen. Gelbes Lufterkennungszeichen auf dem Turmdach. **D2** Die Bedeutung der taktischen Markierungen der Armwinkel und der Geschützlaufstreifen der Israeli wurde niemals bestätigt: verschiedene Kombinationen von diesen identifizieren Bataillone und Kompanien. Die detaillierte Zeichnung zeigt das Zeichen der 7th Armoured Brigade, jedoch nur für Zeremonien angewandt.

E1 Der Panzer ist 'Costa Bower' genannt, ein gälischer Name für eine legendäre 'Todeskutsche'. Das '38B' Abzeichen identifiziert 'C' Sqn.; die Bergungsabteilung ('8'); und die ARV ('B'); '38A' war die Markierung der begleitenden Teilketten fahrzeuge bemannt durch Ingenieure. Die olivgrüne Farbe wurde von dem roten Staub von Vietnam fast total verdeckt. **E2** '31' lässt den Führer 1 Troop, 'C' Sqn. erkennen; das Kanguruh Wappen ist das der 1st Australian Task Force, mit der troop Nummer hinzugefügt. Die grüne Farbe ist bedeckt mit rotem Staub.

F1 Dieser Panzer, in der normalen jordanischen Tarnung von sandgelb und grün, kämpfte gegen die palästinische Befreiungsfront und syrische Truppen. Das rot und gelbe Wappen ist das Abzeichen der 40. Brigade; die kleinen wappen zeigen frühere Arten davon, der linke davon wurde in 1967er Krieg benutzt. **F2** Dieser Panzer war einer von vier, die benutzt wurden um in Ulster Barrikaden einzurammen; bemannt durch die Royal Engineers, er trägt auch das Abzeichen des Schiffes HMS Fearless, welches die Panzer nach Ulster transportierte – die Matrosen befestigten Aufkleber auf den Panzern.

G1 Das individuelle Funkrufzeichen des Panzers 'Aleph-2', ist auf einem befestigten Stück Tuch getragen; die anderen Markierungen sind unerklärt. **G2** Die Markierungen sind unerklärt. Die detaillierte Ansicht zeigt das Mützenabzeichen des Zahal Panzerkorps.

H1 Gemischte britische und amerikanische Kleidung; rotes Taljereep des Regiments; und Divisionsabzeichen auf der Armbinde. **H2** Der Kommandeur des Panzers in der Tafel E1 trägt seine Rangwinkel und den Namen seines Regiments – Royal Australian Electrical and Mechanical Engineers – auf einer Armbinde. **H3** Feuerfeste Überanzüge, und Helme mit inseitiger Radioausstattung, beide von US-Herstellung, von den Israelis kurz vor dem 1973er Krieg erworben. Zwei Rangstreifen an den Offiziers-Schulterklappen zeigen einen Segen – Oberleutnant an. Bemerke die Erkennungsmarken, die um das Fussgelenk anstelle des Halses getragen werden, in Hinsicht auf die schweren Verluste durch Kopfverletzungen in diesem Krieg.